C000118358

McCulloch's Dilemma

Barbara Bryan

Published in 2022

by Barbara Bryan

© Copyright Barbara Bryan

Paperback Edition

ISBN: 978-1-913898-41-0

Cover and Book interior Design by Russell Holden
www.pixeltweakspublications.com

 Pixel Tweaks Publications
SELF PUBLISHING MADE SIMPLE

Thank you to the friends and family
who have helped and encouraged me

It is odd living in a foreign country. A foreign language. A refugee from all that is familiar to me. But at least I am free, and for that I have to be grateful. Others have not been so fortunate. Many have been jailed or waiting to be transported to Botany Bay. And now, as I sit in my lodgings, overlooking a harbour, every day on waking I am reminded of my new environment. For Waalhaven is now my home. Exiled, I have no choice but to live out my life in this alien place. The language has been difficult but a willing hand will always find work, although some are hostile to having a foreigner in their midst. But when I have children, and they are old enough to understand, I will explain the events of my last months in Edinburgh - events that precipitated my exile.

PART ONE

I

6th June 1792, Edinburgh

John was exhausted after his shift working as a typesetter for the *Caledonian Mercury* newspaper in Old Fishmarket Close. The heat in the printing room had been unbearable. The only ventilation was from a metal slated grill, but there had been no draught to alleviate the stifling atmosphere on this still summer's day – only the stench from the fish market at the foot of the close pervaded the room. There was no direct access to water, and fish which were plentiful in the Forth - shellfish, haddock and cod - were dragged to the foot of the narrow close by boys and sold from old, rickety, wooden tables encrusted with fish scales. At the end of the trading day, a residue of rotting fish heads and innards was left to decompose on the cobbled close. A welcome feast for animals - an abhorrent aroma for humans. But John had been keen to accept the job as a typesetter on the *Caledonian Mercury*, and, having an easy disposition, he knew his senses would, in time, become accustomed to the stinking smell. And they had. After a few months, he barely noticed it.

He wiped the sweat off the top half of his torso, put his shirt on, bid his colleague goodbye and stepped into the dingy close, the sun being obscured by the tall tenements. An attractive youth, with a pleasant demeanour, John felt particularly pleased with himself that day because Mr Brechin, the proprietor of the newspaper, had told him he was going to be rewarded for his good work and have his salary raised from a shilling and sixpence, to two shillings a week. He had arrived in the city to start his typesetting apprenticeship when he was thirteen and now, five years later, he felt he was beginning to progress.

He turned into the High Street and started to stroll down the hill to his lodgings. The High Street was strewn with debris from the riot of two days before: discarded pamphlets, dried blood encrusted in the grooves of the cobbles. Every year there was a riotous assembly on the High Street to celebrate the King's birthday on the fourth of June. It was an Edinburgh tradition. But this year had been different. The crowd had a distinct purpose, to give vent to their anger for Lord Henry Dundas – the uncrowned King Harry the ninth of Scotland and Home Secretary under the Pitt government – was again opposing Richard Sheridan's motion to form a Committee of Inquiry to investigate the veracity of the Burgesses allegations that abuses were endemic amongst the Magistrates in the Royal Burghs of Scotland. Self-elected, Magistrates were accountable to no-one and thousands of Burgesses had petitioned Parliament over the past five years seeking redress for these abuses and asked Parliament to set up annual elections to be vested in the community. Dundas denied there were any abuses and kept on opposing Sheridan's motions with excuses such as lack of evidence, that the motion was raised too early or too late in the Parliamentary session.

The crowd were also angry at the King's recent proclamation banning the publication of pamphlets being attached to public boards throughout the land promoting the rights to equality for all men – pamphlets precipitated by Thomas Paine's revelatory comments in his recently published book 'The Rights of Man'. "*Citizens we must rebel against the tyranny of power usurped*" … "*An army of principles can penetrate, where an army of soldiers cannot*" … "*We have in our power to begin the world over again.*" There were many more provocative statements which Dundas, in the House of Commons, termed 'inflammatory and seditious writings.' The following day, the King issued his proclamation.

King George III went even further and stated it would now be a criminal offence for anyone caught printing, publishing or distributing any of what he called 'seditious material', and he commanded all Magistrates to notify the Home Secretary, Lord Henry Dundas, of anyone who was involved in this activity. But banning the book inevitably increased its popularity. Scotland had a literate population and Paine's sentiments that the money paid in taxes should be used for the benefit of the population - education, child benefit, pensions for the elderly and poor relief – was a revelation. People were sick to death of the stranglehold Dundas and his cronies had over the voting system in the Burghs. Bribery and corruption meant there was no fair representation in Parliament. Those in power, retained their power and the interests of others was disregarded. Paine highlighted the fact that only a fraction of the people in Britain who paid taxes were entitled to vote – an attitude that mirrored the discontent about the voting system in the Burghs.

On the day of the King's birthday, towards early evening, John heard a commotion outside. He worked near Parliament House where the Magistrates and local dignitaries were drinking his Majesty's health. When he eventually got onto the High Street, magistrates had spilled out onto the street, dead cats were lying all over the place (flinging dead cats around on the King's birthday was a tradition) and troops were everywhere. A huge crowd of men were rampaging down the High Street shouting, 'Doon wi' Dundas'. Flinging bottles, stones and sticks into shop windows, they were disregarding the troops who were trying to surround the area, their bayonets glistening in the evening sun. Soldiers on horseback were trying to control the crowd, but their efforts were thwarted by the squibs and crackers being thrown at the beasts, who started in terror as the soldiers yanked in the reins tightly to stop them from bolting. Men, women and children, residents in the tall tenements in the High Street, were hanging out of their windows shouting at the soldiers and goading the mob to do more damage. Stones were being flung at the soldiers from six storeys high. Some soldiers succeeded in deflecting them with their bodies, others were not so fortunate as they tumbled to the ground, blood pouring from wounds. In the distance, John saw smoke spiraling up into the sky. "They've set fire tae a sentry box," a man shouted from one of the windows. The crowd cheered. Soldiers started to run down the hill, towards the chaos. A magistrate beside John, arms gesticulating wildly, bellowed to a soldier on horseback, "Git the firemaster". John watched at a distance. The fire was eventually quenched, the mob's rage abated and, as the soldiers started to clear the streets, John felt it safe to go back to his lodgings at the far end of the High Street.

Two days later, as he ambled down the road, apart from the debris, the High Street had returned to normal. Traders were returning home with their goods. Beggars stood on corners hoping to have some left over produce thrown to them and men were emerging from the dingy taverns. He could hear a drum beating in the distance. He stopped, cocked his head to one side, and listened. It wasn't the beat or regular rhythmic roll of an army drum. It was a constant, pulsating beat resonating from a bass drum. Curious, John continued on.

A stifling summer evening, as he meandered down the High Street, he saw a procession of men and women crossing the High Street at the Tron Kirk, making their way down North Bridge. John could hear them singing above the drum beat. When he reached the Tron Kirk, glancing to his right and left all he could see was a mass of marching heads. There were no magisterial gowns present, only ordinary tradespeople and labour men. And John, reticent by nature, thought it was such a jovial atmosphere he spontaneously decided to join them and got into step with the crowd and asked a stranger next to him:

"Whaur are ye gaun?"

"Tae the Lord Provost's house in St Andrew Square."

"Why?"

"Tae protest aboot Dundas."

John had seen the handbills. *'Burn the villain Dundas'*; *'Now is the time/ Burn the villain/ Fear not – All will be supported.'* He hesitated for a moment, deliberating whether he should stay with the crowd or just go back to his lodgings, but it was such a convivial atmosphere he decided to continue on.

More drums started beating as they approached their destination. John estimated there must have been two thousand people milling around St Andrew Square. He had never seen anything like it. He had known about the unrest. His paper had published the debate in the House of Commons; the proclamation and the growing hatred of Dundas who was using his authority to suppress the people, but it had never occurred to him to get involved. This evening was an adventure for him. He was elated by the atmosphere, the great sense of camaraderie. Pamphlets were being handed out. John took one and quickly read it. "Down with Dundas and his despotic government." A man was hoisted onto someone's shoulders near the house and brandishing a pamphlet shouted out. "Doon wi' Dundas! The King has issued a proclamation which mist be ignored." The crowd erupted into a mighty roar and chanted in unison, "Doon wi' Dundas!" Then, amidst the rabble, two guns were heard being fired from the castle. The crowd reacted. Houses were being built in the square and people started to pick up stones from the rubble and hurl them at the windows of the Lord Provost's house. When one shattered, the crowd roared in approval. The man who was elevated at the front of the crowd, close to the house, shouted in glee and goaded people to throw more stones. The noise became deafening when several of the windows shattered simultaneously. John joined in the atmosphere, brandishing his pamphlet. "Git the sentry boxes," someone shouted out. Two sentry boxes were positioned near the house and the next thing John saw was them being lifted up and carried to the front of the house. "Break 'em up," he heard a man shout. The protest swelled when the crowd heard the command, and people surged forward towards the house. Squashed by the throng of people surrounding him, and enthralled by the atmosphere, John felt compelled to join in the sea of voices.

Suddenly he heard another voice shout from behind. "Sodjers!" He turned his head and saw raised bayonet blades coming towards them. The mood immediately disintegrated, replaced with fear and panic. He could see soldiers starting to cordon people in the crowd and attack them with their bayonet butts. They were rapidly approaching where John stood. One noticed John had a pamphlet in his hand. He pushed people aside, immediately rushed over to him and grabbed his arm. John struggled frantically to get rid of him then, suddenly, he felt a searing pain in his head. The soldier had struck him with his bayonet butt. 'Run!" he heard people shout, but, being mildly concussed, John could not react immediately although he was aware of the crowd rapidly trying to disperse. He was still clutching the pamphlet in his hand and heard another soldier's voice shout out in his direction, "Git that yin!" Two soldiers were now coming towards him. He instantly reacted. Pushing people aside he started ducking and diving, running as fast as he could to get to North St David Street at the side of the Lord Provost's house. "Stop!" he heard one of the soldiers calling out. He ignored him and continued sprinting as hard as he could.

II

At the foot of the street he sped towards a drying green opposite and beyond that an orchard. Terrified he would be caught, he endured the pulsating pain in his head when he had to duck to avoid branches. He knew he couldn't stop until he could no longer hear the soldier's voices. Further into the orchard he ran, determined to escape. He had been running for what appeared to be ages and started to feel dizzy. He stopped for a moment and listened. Nothing. Silence. They must have given up the chase. Though he was relieved, his dilemma was – where could he go? He couldn't go back to his lodgings as that would mean crossing North Bridge and there were bound to be soldiers on guard looking out for those who had been at St Andrew Square. And with his obvious head wound, which he couldn't disguise, they would immediately recognise him as being part of the crowd.

He decided to wait a little longer and crouched in the undergrowth. He needed time to think; to compose himself; to decide what would be the next best course of action. The flow of blood had fortunately abated but his shirt was stained with it. Then he remembered his Aunt was the cook at Lord Hugh's house at the far end of Queen Street. Following the paths through orchards, he could seek refuge there. It was now late in the evening and the sun was setting as he stealthily made his way towards the house. As he got closer to it, he glanced back in the direction of St Andrew Square, about a quarter of a mile away. The street was deserted. But he was conspicuous with his blooded clothes and thought it auspicious to wait until darkness fell. He was still clutching the pamphlet and had to get rid of it. He dug a hole with his hands in the dry earth and successfully concealed it.

His body was recovering from the exertion of fleeing and he sat down and waited patiently for the right time to bolt to the house. When the sun set he was relieved there was not a full moon in the sky because, if he was careful, he could arrive at the house undetected before his aunt retired for the evening. He stood up. Still no-one was visible and not a sound could be heard. When he arrived at the house, the first-floor drawing room window was illuminated. He scurried down the stone stairs, but before he reached the bottom he stopped and glimpsed into the kitchen window. His aunt was the only person present - the kitchen and scullery maid had obviously retired - and she was cleaning copper pans in readiness for the forthcoming day's meals. He approached the door, glanced surreptitiously over his shoulder to determine he wasn't observed, and tapped it twice gently. Nothing. He tapped again, trying to suppress the anxiety that was starting to well up. He put his ear to the door and listened for the sound of footsteps on the flag stones. Silence. What should he do? He couldn't knock any louder for fear of attracting attention in the drawing room. Finally, after another attempt, he heard his aunt's footsteps approaching. "Who's there?" she asked in a loud whisper.

"It's John," he whispered back. "Yer nephew."

She rapidly unlocked the door and when she saw the state he was in with his tousled hair and shirt encased in dried blood she spontaneously cried out: "Guid Lord! What in God's name has happened tae ye?" and ushered him quickly into the kitchen, locking the door behind.

In a low voice, suffused with anxiety, he recounted the tale, imploring her to believe he wasn't one of the ringleaders. When he had finished she earnestly looked at him and said, "I believe ye." Her mood changed. "We've got tae get ye cleaned up. Gimme yer shirt," and pointing to a stool at the far end of the kitchen told him to sit down on it. Taking the shirt, she said "I'll be back in a meenit," and went out of the kitchen clutching it in her hand.

John sat bemused on the stool. He couldn't believe what had happened. And if Mr Brechin found out he had been at the riot that would put an end to any future prospects he had at the paper. But he managed to quell his panic by persuading himself that nobody would know. The people in the crowd were complete strangers. He would never meet them again. It would be all right.

His aunt came back, walked over to the stove and draped the wet shirt over the top rail. She turned to look at him and said, "It'll be dry by the time ye leave."

"Thank ye" he replied, then hastily added. "Naebody maun ken I wis here."

"Of course not" his aunt agreed.

"An'," he anxiously continued, I cannae go back tae ma lodgings the nicht. Sodjers will still be aboot. I cannae risk it."

A practical woman, she immediately came up with a solution. "I can pit ye in the china closet fur a few oors. I'm the only one wi a key. Ye'll be fine," she reassured him and, picking up a kettle from the stove, she took a bowl from a shelf nearby and filled it with warm water. Placing it on the counter, she went to a drawer, retrieved a cloth, came back to him, ripped it in half, and started to wash the blood from his face. Then she parted his hair at the back and examined the wound. "It's nae that deep. I'll pit some Balaggan's salve on afore ye leave. That'll help heal the wound quickly. Fortunately, ye've got a guid head o' thick hair tae cover it." She went to another drawer, took out some lint, retrieved another cloth, dipped that in oil and returned to him. "This might hurt a little, bit it hae tae be done." He could feel her opening the wound and placing the soft lint inside, then she covered it with the cloth dipped in oil and put the remaining cloth around his head as a bandage. After she had finished she said abruptly, "Follow me".

He got off the stool and followed her out of the kitchen into the corridor where she stopped outside a door to the left, chose a key from a ring of keys secured around her waist by a thick leather belt and opened the door. John stepped inside. A small, windowless room, it had shelves on either side of the walls laden with beautiful china – dinner services with stunning, vivid patterns the like of which he had never seen. On the floor was a stout wooden chest, a perfect seat. "I'll bring a blanket tae wrap around ye." She closed the door and he sat down on the chest. He could hear her footsteps on the corridor and then a female voice. "Hello Mrs MacPherson. I was just checking all was prepared for the morning."

"Aye Miss Amelia," he heard his aunt respond. "Aw' done as usual."

Amelia, sure she had heard voices coming from the kitchen, looked back in that direction and noticed the shirt draped over the rail. She decided not to comment, wished Mrs MacPherson good night and proceeded back up the stairs. A few minutes later the door opened and his aunt handed him the blanket. She whispered, "I'll be back afore dawn" and left, turning the key in the lock.

As soon as she had gone, he leant his back against the wall and began to think of Amelia. Lord Hugh's daughter. He hadn't seen her in years, not since he had started his apprenticeship with Mr Brechin at the *Caledonian Mercury*. It was Amelia's father who had recommended him to the proprietor of the newspaper. And he started to reminisce – back to the first day he met her.

His father was the gamekeeper on Lord Hugh's estate near Penicuik and when he was seven he had been allowed to roam the forest in the summer holidays. It had a great choice of trees to climb – oak, ash, birch, hazel, elm, beech, sycamore – and he loved to see how far he could get – the top being the goal, but that often was unobtainable. His father had taken him into the forest frequently when he was little and shown him tracks from various animals – roe deer, lynx, foxes, red squirrels, goshawks and wild cats. One day, he was following the tracks of a badger when he came upon a tall, stone wall. There was an arch to the right of it with a wrought iron gate covered in mesh to keep the rabbits out. He went over and opened the gate – carefully closing it after him. It was the kitchen garden of the big house. Nobody was there and John, completely engrossed in the vision of such a variety of produce before him, never thought to glance round as he entered someone else's property. His family had a small plot of land attached to their cottage where they grew their own vegetables – potatoes, turnips, carrots - which he sometimes helped his father weed, but he had never seen such variety. Divided by grass paths, it was huge with row upon row of flourishing vegetables he didn't recognise. In the corner, on the left hand side, was a large dung heap and at the top of the garden was a vast glass house. To his right was a collection of fruit trees, with branches bending towards the ground laden with apples, cherries, pears.

As he was meandering down a row, he stopped, bent down and touched an unfamiliar vegetable. It had an abundance of leaves and, curious to see if it was soft inside, prodded the middle and then heard a young voice behind him say: "What are doing? Are you thinking of stealing it?" Affronted, he turned his head to see who had spoken. It was a girl, about his age, dressed in a pink and white floral dress, wearing white satin shoes, secured by a pink ribbon bound round her ankle in a bow at the back. Her golden hair was tied in long pigtails. He stood up and indignantly responded. "Of course not!"

She mellowed. "What's your name?" she asked.

"John McCulloch," he sulkily replied.

"Well John McCulloch" she haughtily responded. "I bet you can't run as fast I can," and she immediately started to sprint down the path towards the glass house.

"Oh aye I can," he eagerly retorted and went chasing after her. That was the beginning of their friendship.

III

They were seven years old and every day in that summer holiday, the first of many, they would meet early afternoon once Amelia had finished her studies with her governess, Miss Pringle. They would rendezvous at the wrought iron gate and decide what adventure they would get involved with that day. She had never explored the forest on her own and, following in his father's footsteps, he enjoyed teaching her how to identify the tracks of the animals living in the wooded environment. Like him, she loved nature and delighted in learning about the wild life on their estate. She loved riding and persuaded Joe, the groom, to teach him how to ride. John encouraged her to climb trees and showed her how to balance on the branches. She always wore dresses and frequently the material would get caught up in a branch and occasionally rip but she didn't care, it all added to the pleasure of finding a new playmate. And she loved the freedom, being away from the confines of the discipline of studying.

She introduced John to Bob, the head gardener. A stocky man in his mid-fifties, he had started as a garden apprentice when he was sixteen and had been there ever since, building up the produce in the kitchen garden. The summers were predictably warm and he was always bare chested, exposing his bronzed body and bulging muscles. Wearing stout boots, his breeches were tied up with string. He took John to the hothouse where he grew exotic fruits – melons, grapes and pineapples – and in the kitchen garden he allowed them to help him gather the fruit when it ripened. They each had a wicker basket and he showed them how to carefully remove delicate fruits, like raspberries, so as not to damage them when they plucked them from the branches. There were apple trees and bushes laden with black currants, redcurrants, white currants, strawberries and gooseberries which were the most difficult to pluck because of the thorns surrounding the fruit. The raspberries though were mouth-watering and of course they were tempted to eat them, which they did in abundance. Sometimes the juice would dribble onto one of her pretty dresses and if his aunt noticed the stain, she would gently scold her for giving the washing-girl extra work.

Once the baskets were full, they would make their way to the kitchen in the big house where his aunt Agnes was cook. They would help her wash the fruit which would eventually be put into jars and made into the most delicious jams. With jam preserved from the year before she would make scones for them to eat and they would sit around the large oak kitchen table and gorge themselves.

Towards the end of the summer they would go with Bob to the orchard where branches were heavy with ripe apples. He had a special stick he sometimes let them use to nudge the apples free. Often John would use the stick and Amelia would catch the apples as they dropped to the ground. When it was time for Amelia to go back for supper, his aunt would stand in the courtyard outside the kitchen door and vigorously ring a huge brass bell to alert Amelia it was time to finish play for the day and come back to the house. It was astonishing how far the noise of the bell travelled.

At the end of the holidays they would part and he would return to school and await the winter and predictable chest colds he developed every year. He could barely remember a winter in his youth when he was not confined to bed. As soon as the dark nights enveloped them, so did the cold and damp and that had him laid up in bed, sometimes for weeks. His aunt was adept at making up remedies for various ailments. A great number of herbs were grown in the kitchen garden and, to help his cough, she would give his mother a large bunch of feltwort, the leaves of which would be hung up to dry in their cottage. When he became ill his mother would boil up water, put two teaspoons of the dried leaves into the hot water, strain it and give him the tea. His aunt had also recommended mixing honey with pepper to alleviate the coughing.

It was preferable to stay in bed because there was no fire in the room. The smoke from their kitchen fire made his symptoms much worse. But the predictable time spent in what he considered to be solitary confinement was pleasant for him. It was a relief not to go to school for many weeks in the winter as the walk there involved trudging two miles over rugged frosty paths. And because of his 'delicate' state', it meant he didn't have to endure any bullying from the boys. It also meant he didn't have to go to the Sunday church services – one in the morning, and one in the afternoon. But he still had religious instruction even when he was ill as his father would spend a great deal of time on the Sabbath reading passages from the King James Bible.

His father was a literate man and introduced John to a love of reading. When he was ill in bed, his father would read to him. "Books are a great thing son. Ye can be transported tae magical places." And indeed he was. Robinson Crusoe was a book he loved, being immersed in an adventure in a foreign environment, and once he had learned to read, being confined to bed with a book was a luxury. There was a small library of books at school, contributed by Lord Hugh. His teacher, Mr Ford, a kind man, was delighted he was such an enthusiastic reader and periodically would walk to their cottage on a Saturday to deliver yet another book.

He recalled the second summer he and Amelia had spent together. Towards the end of the holiday they were sitting at the kitchen table when Amelia announced, "My father would like to meet you." John felt abashed at the prospect of meeting a Lord and he blushed from the tip of his toes to the top of his head. Amelia, noticing his face turn deep red with embarrassment, frivolously said, "Don't be so silly John. He's not an ogre," and promptly got up from her chair and declared, "We're going to visit him now."

He had no choice but to follow her out of the kitchen. It was the first time they had ventured into the heart of the big house. She marched ahead of him and they entered the main entrance hall. He stopped, awestruck with the vision. It was vast with a huge ornate carved wooden fireplace; gilt edged framed paintings and portraits adorned the walls and the sonorous ticking of the brass pendulum in the longcase clock resonated throughout. His eyes wandered upwards as he marvelled at the beautifully carved beams in the ceiling. Amelia, oblivious to her familiar opulent surroundings, had already proceeded to bounce up the grand spiral staircase jauntily, calling out, "C'mon John." He hastily followed her admiring the life-sized oil painted portraits of ancestors adorning the walls on the landing. When they reached the top of the stairs, she said, "We're going to the library," and proceeded to skip along a carpeted corridor, lined with oak carved doors. She stopped at one, and knocked. "Come in my dear," he heard a male voice respond.

She opened the door and they entered. Her father was seated at a large desk by the window. He greeted her with open arms and she immediately rushed over to him, sat on his lap and embraced his neck with a big hug. John was stunned, overawed by the volume of books laden on the shelves surrounding the room. He had never seen so many in his life before. At school there was only a small selection of books but in this room there must have been thousands. Completely engrossed in the pleasure of seeing so much reading material he barely heard Lord Hugh's voice say to his daughter. "Is this the young man you play with my dear?" But he heard Amelia's voice harshly call out, "John! Don't be so rude."

He turned round. Amelia was cuddled in her father's lap. He adored his daughter. She was the apple of his eye. But John was mortified. He had been brought up to respect adults, and was acutely aware that he did not speak like Amelia or her father. "I'm sorry sir," he mumbled with his head bowed.

"Come over here my boy," her father responded. As John, head still bowed, shyly walked towards the desk he remembered a conversation at home when his father was discussing Lord Hugh with his mother. He had said to her what a good landlord Lord Hugh was and that he was very considerate toward his tenants and workers He stood in front of the desk. "What is your name young man?" Lord Hugh asked.

"John McCulloch sir."

"And you like reading?"

Animated at having the opportunity to talk about his passion John looked up and responded, "Oh aye sir!" And with his favourite subject on his lips, he continued, "Very much sir. When I'm ill in the winter sir, my teacher brings me books to read."

The old man chuckled and smiled benignly at his daughter. "Maybe you'll encourage my daughter to read a little more."

"Father, don't scold."

"I wouldn't do that dearest," and he gently lifted her off his knee and put her down on the carpet. He rose from his chair, picked up his spectacles which were lying on the desk surrounded by papers, and addressing John, asked, "Have you read Gulliver's Travels?"

"No sir."

"Well then, we'll have to find you a copy," and he purposefully strode over to a specific shelf. John was still rooted in the same standing position as Lord Hugh put on his spectacles and started to browse the titles on the shelf. A moment later, he retrieved a book and walked over to John. "There you are my young man," he said as he handed John the leather bound copy "I hope you enjoy it. Now my dearest," he said turning to his daughter "I must continue with my work. Off you go and play." He bent down to give her a peck on the cheek, which she returned, and they left the room.

IV

John's reverie was interrupted when he heard the key turn in the lock and his aunt entered the china closet. "It's three o'clock," she whispered. "Ye mist get gaun. Come." He followed her to the kitchen. She pointed at the stool. "Sit doon there. I'll check the wound."

He sat on the stool as she unravelled the bandage and gently removed the lint to examine the wound. To his relief she announced, "It's healing nicely. Ye'll no need the bandage. I'll put on the salve an' gie ye a little tae tak awa wi ye. Apply it on the wound twice a day for the next three days. Wi' that thick head o' hair, the scar wilnae be noticed."

While she was getting the salve and his shirt John felt compelled to ask: "How is Amelia? I heard her talking tae ye last night."

"She's training tae be a lady," his aunt responded. "She's very busy these days and Lord Hugh is keen fur her tae learn aboot households as she'll have yin o' her ain tae manage hersel when she gits mairret."

Startled, John asked, "Is she getting mairret?"

"No yet," his aunt replied, "but she's a pretty girl, an' it'll no be lang afore someone asks fr her hand." She came over and as she began to gently rub the salve into the wound he felt moved to tell her about his reminiscences. "When I wis in the closet I wis thinking aboot the times we used tae play thegither."

"Och," said his aunt matter-of-factly, "that wis a lang time ago. She'll no be remembering those days. Noo," she said, handing him his shirt and a little jar of salve, "ye mist leave."

He got up and they walked to the door. She unlocked it. He embraced her, said, "Thank ye," and left.

It was still dark. The sun would not be rising for another hour. He tiptoed up the stairs and, when he reached the top, furtively looked to his left and right. No person was visible and so without hesitation, he sprinted back down to the feued plots, sought shelter amidst the orchards, and ran till he reached the end at the far side of St Andrew Square. He stopped and took a few moments to catch his breath. The next stage was going to be difficult because once he got onto the street, he would be exposed. He quietly got to the edge of an orchard then stood still and listened for the sound of voices. Nothing. That didn't mean there was no-one around because there would be sentries stationed in the square but, he surmised, there shouldn't be anybody at the back of Thomas Dundas' house or, he hoped, at the side of Register House. Once he got there, he could run to the lee of North Bridge and make his way back to his lodgings.

He had to get going before dawn rose so, feeling a sense of urgency, started creeping amongst the rubble surrounding the area. He successfully got to the back of the Dundas residence and had just reached the side of Register House when he heard a voice call out, "Wha goes there?" He froze momentarily, then dropped flat on his stomach amongst the rubble. His heart was beating so loudly he thought whoever it was would hear it. With a great effort he quelled his breathing and lay as still as he possibly could. He heard footsteps nearby. They stopped. Then a moment later receded. He waited, still prone on the ground. He realised he couldn't make a run to the lee of North Bridge, for if he crossed directly over to the Canongate side he would be exposed and possibly seen by a soldier. He would have to circumvent it and go up towards the Bridewell, the new prison built near Calton Hill. Much ground had to be excavated whilst it was being built so he could seek shelter amongst the rocks and turf and then stealthily make his way to the bridge.

He quietly set off. Pitch black, he frequently stumbled on rocks and damaged his shins but at length he got to the flat ground and slid along his belly till he reached the lee of North Bridge. It would be a slippery slope clambering up the embankment at the far end of North Bridge, but he knew he could manage that. Once at the top though he would have to be on the lookout for the night Town Guards, the stocky Highlanders who would be roaming the city after the riot, keen to brandish their Lochaber axes in the direction of any person creeping around at that time of night.

He had almost reached the top of the embankment without encountering anyone, when he stumbled over a body on the ground. It was a sleeping beggar. Startled, the beggar let out a wild roar thinking someone was about to attack him. John, terrified the voice would alert one of the Town Guards, immediately dropped down to his knees to pacify the man and assure him he was not an assailant. Once done, he remained crouched, his senses alive, listening out for the sound of footsteps coming in their direction responding to the beggar's roar. He waited, and waited. Nothing.

The first flecks of dawn were visible in the sky. He heard the clock at St Giles strike a quarter to four. He must hurry to get back to his lodgings before Mr MacFadyen arose at four to start his shift at Scott's bakery in Forrester's Wynd, near the Lawnmarket. Still crouching, he carefully manoeuvred his way to the top of the embankment. Their tenement was near the Tron Kirk, only minutes away. He stood up, looked in every direction, saw nobody, and made a dash for the entrance to his close. Once there, he crept up the stone stairs to the top floor, quietly opened the door and listened out for Mr MacFadyen's snores, coming from the bed recess in the kitchen. He took a step forward with every snore, got to his boxroom, adjacent to the kitchen, opened the door and finally, lay down on his bed.

No sooner had he collapsed onto his bed he heard Mr MacFadyen up and about cooking his oatmeal breakfast before he started his shift. John knew he would soon depart, but despite the fact he was exhausted, he knew sleep would elude him after all the anxiety of the past few hours and he started to recall when he had first arrived in the city.

He would have loved to have followed in his father's footsteps but Lord Hugh wasn't employing anyone else on the estate and, with John's love of reading, he had offered to contact Mr Brechin, the proprietor of the *Caledonian Mercury*, and get him a job as an apprentice typesetter on the paper. Mr Brechin had organised his lodging with the MacFadyen family, who couldn't have made him feel more welcome. Mrs MacFadyen was a kindly soul, with a round, full face and laughing eyes. Small in stature, she worked in one of the krame stalls selling pots and pans.

But he remembered the difficulty he had in adjusting to the claustrophobic atmosphere of the city when he first arrived. Coming from the peace and quiet and open space of the country, his senses were assaulted as soon as he had alighted the coach at the Ramsay Inn, in St Mary's Wynd. The smell of human waste. Crowds of people. Rotting rubbish strewn everywhere. Towering tenements, obscuring the sunlight. But he had no choice but to soak up the atmosphere of the crowds, the range of people bustling about the closes, the vegetable markets, with drunken, gin-soaked elderly women selling the produce. And the beggars. He had never seen a beggar before. Never seen such ragged people. It had never occurred to him that people did not have a home to go to, had no job, and were scrabbling around for food, looking for scraps to eat. He remembered he had had to typeset a notice from the Town Council saying the city was '*infested with idle, vagrant begging poor from all parts of the country. The Lord Provost and Magistrates have given strictest orders to the superintendent of the Police, Sergeants and soldiers of the City Guard, Cadies, Porters etc. to apprehend and commit them to Thieves Hole Vaults in the North bridge.*

They'll be confined with only bread and water and if found still loitering about the city they'll be confined again and severely punished.' There was thieving and illicit stills in the city, but the Town Guards who patrolled the streets kept a lot of criminal activity at bay.

In the first few months, he didn't explore the city. He remembered he felt vulnerable and when he left his lodgings he would walk resolutely straight up the High Street to Fishmarket Close. He had to pass many beggars and while that distressed him to begin with like everything in the city he gradually adapted to the atmosphere.

He stopped reminiscing when he heard the children in the kitchen, blethering and gobbling their oatmeal and light ale breakfast before they started school at seven. Once they had noisily departed, he waited a few minutes till the St Giles clock struck the hour. It was time to go, but before he left his room, he gently felt his wound. The salve his aunt had put on had worked miraculously, it had almost healed. As a precaution, he took the little jar from his pocket and massaged a small amount on the wound, covering it up with his thick hair. Although he couldn't see the back of his head, he was sure it was sufficiently camouflaged. Then he changed his shirt, paranoid that he might be recognised from the night before. He usually had breakfast with Mrs MacFadyen and the children but he wasn't in the mood for speaking to anyone, and calling out to Mrs MacFadyen, "I've git an early start," he rushed out of the door.

He left the tenement, turned right and started to walk towards the Tron. When he reached North Bridge, his heart started to pound in panic. A group of soldiers were gathered there, obviously looking for any stray rioters coming up the steps from Fleshmarket Close. He had to subdue the urge to flee and attempted to appear as nonchalant as possible. As he approached the group, he was aware that one of the soldiers were glancing in his direction and, remembering being chased the night before, he thought he might be recognised and hear him shout out, 'Stop!" But he maintained a steady pace, focusing all his attention on the fruit market tables beyond the group. He didn't slacken his pace and was so relieved no call came. Further on towards his work, he passed a town guard standing outside the Tolbooth prison, then the krames, Creech's Land and … Old Fleshmarket Close. At the foot of the close fish wives had set up their tables but apart from them, it was deserted. He breathed a huge sigh of relief and opened the door.

When he entered the typesetting room, his colleague James, was already sitting at his bench working away. Surprised, he looked up at John and announced, "Yer early." Then he chortled, "It's as if hauf the toun wiz up at dawn the day efter last nicht's riot."

Feigning ignorance John asked, as casually as possible. "Whit riot?"

"Did ye no hear the racket?"

"No," he lied, "I went tae ma bed early."

"Did ye no hear the guns being fired frae the castle? How could ye no hae heard them?"

John sat down on his bench with his back deliberately to James in case his face disclosed any lie. He didn't respond but James rapidly continued, "That was tae bring up the Marines frae Leith. They say there were twa thoosan folk a' headed towards St Andrew Square.

Mind we printed an article aboot the Magistrates warning people they would tak action efter the King's Birthday riot? Weel, they alerted the army and the 53rd foot regiment wiz on the grund tae quell ony problems. They marched tae St Andrew Square. Seventeen folk hae been arrested. They're in the Tolbooth. And the sodgers are still peepin' oot fur people."

John felt moved to make a comment. "I saw sodgers on my way here, at the top end o' North Bridge...."

" Aye," James eagerly responded. "They're still looking fur some o' them. I wouldn't like tae be held in the Tolbooth prison, cooped up in this infernal heat, an' nae chance o' a fair trial, should ye git yin. And if you did, there wid be every chance ye'd be ordered tae languish in prison for months." He tapped John on the shoulder and asked, "Whit dae ye think aboot the ither riots that hae recently happened?"

"I dinnae want tae git involved,"

"Aye. Bit do ye no think the grievances are fair? We ought tae hae a better voting system so them that have sae much can at least consider whit we common people need." He turned round to face his typesetting blocks. "Ye mist hae seen the handbills?" he continued. "They wur strewn a' ower the toun. '*Burn the villain Dundas*.'"

"Aye," replied John, still stooped over his bench. "Bit I didnae tak' ony notice o' them."

"Well ye should hae!"

Cautious as ever, John thought it auspicious for them not to be discussing anything about the atmosphere in town and said in a firm voice, "Ye shuid be careful. If

Mr Brechin heard ye talking like that, he might report ye tae the authorities an' ye cuid end up in the Tolbooth."

"I dinnae think so," James frivolously retorted. "I'm only saying whit's on a'body's lips the noo."

"That may be," said John, picking up his composing stick and settling into his shift, "bit I suggest ye keep yer thoughts tae yersel."

V

Iona, the kitchenmaid, wouldn't have heeded John's words. She felt honoured that day because Mrs MacPherson had asked her, "Jist the once mind," to go to the Flesh Market. When she had got there at seven in the morning, the market was packed with people, all talking about the riot of the night before. Not a gossip by nature, Iona's ears were flapping as she heard the women animatedly discussing what had happened and the number of arrests. As she scampered back carrying the fare for the day, she was brimming over with excitement in anticipation of telling Mrs MacPherson the news she had heard and arrived at the kitchen door in a breathless state. Agnes was standing at the stove, stirring a sauce and immediately turned round when Iona came in, "Whit's the maiter?" she asked.

Iona, still trying to catch her breath, started to splutter out the news just as Meg, Amelia's maid, entered the kitchen. "An' seventeen people hae been arrested."

Stunned, Agnes immediately thought John had been picked up on his way back to his lodgings. "Dae ye ken whae they are?" she asked.

"I only heard yin name"

Agnes' heart missed a beat. "Whae's?"

"John Taylor" Iona quickly responded. "He's an assistant tae a brewer's servant."

Agnes turned her attention back to the stove and began to vigorously stir the sauce.

"Aye," continued Iona, still excited by what she had heard, "an' the sodjers are still at North Bridge keekin oot fur mair."

How would Agnes know if John had been arrested? She couldn't mention it to anyone and there was no way she could get a message to him. What a dilemma! She'd have to pray he was safe. That was the only thing she could do. And she must compose herself. Still stirring, she asked Iona, who by this time had calmed herself down. "Whit wis the riot aboot?"

"They were sayin it wis tae dae wi' voting reform. Bit I didnae understand whit they were talkin aboot"

"Well. It's ower noo," Agnes curtly responded. "Ye best get yersel upstairs an' attend tae yer work. Yer a'ready a wee bit late."

Meg, standing by the kitchen door looked animated and said, "That's something exciting happening in the city."

"Aye," responded Iona excitedly. "It surely is."

"Nae mair 'o this talk noo," said Agnes, and turning her glance to Meg asked, "Is it something fur Miss Amelia yer wantin'?"

"Aye," Meg replied. "She'd like a ewer o' warm water."

"Well then," said Agnes to Iona, "away an' git the water fur Miss Amelia."

"Aye," Iona meekly responded and did as she was told.

"I shouldn't trouble Miss Amelia wi' whit's happened in the city," Mrs MacPherson had told Meg as she was leaving. Meg of course immediately recounted the tale. Amelia had heard the guns being fired from the castle but had presumed it was a continuation of the King's Birthday celebrations. No doubt all would be revealed at dinner on Saturday when William came, her brother Malcolm's best friend. In the meantime she and Meg discussed her agenda for the day.

A sedan chair would arrive at ten forty-five to take her to her weekly art class at the Ladies Drawing Academy at the West side of St Bridge Street. Mr Walker ran the classes where he set up still life for drawing and painting. There was just a small group of young ladies, six in total, but it was a good intimate atmosphere for them to practise their hobby. Amelia had set up an easel in a nursery room at the top of their house. It afforded a wonderful view of the Firth of Forth and beyond to Fife. The light in the sky was ever changing and she found the peace and quiet inspiring for the painting work. She knew she wasn't an authority in the craft, but it gave her immense pleasure mixing her watercolours, trying to capture the ever-changing visual panoramas.

Then at six thirty, two sedan chairs were going to arrive to take her and her father to a concert at St Cecilia's Hall which started at seven. When they had first arrived in Edinburgh the previous autumn, they found it was easier for each to go in a sedan chair rather than a carriage as it was a steep hill down to the Cowgate and in inclement weather it was difficult for horses' hooves to get a grip on the cobbles, so they continued their sedan tradition even in the summer.

Situated in Niddry Street, just off the Cowgate, St Cecilia's Hall was the first purpose-built concert hall in Scotland. But five years previously, when South Bridge was being built, several closes had been demolished in the process, including Niddry's Wynd, which had been the original entrance, with an elegant courtyard and portico entrance to a grand foyer. Now, concertgoers had to travel down a narrow street and enter through a nondescript door into the foyer and attendances had started to diminish with the building of the new Assembly Rooms in George Street.

However, this evening being the last performance of the season, the foyer, with its double staircase leading to the concert hall on the first floor, was packed. Amelia and her father acknowledged familiar faces and then went upstairs. An elegant oval shaped hall with an elliptical ceiling, and a domed cupola in the centre, it had perfect acoustics. Seating, for four hundred at a squeeze, was on five tiered covered benches on either side of the walls. In the middle, was a vacant oval shaped space, enabling concertgoers to rendezvous with friends and acquaintances during the interval. And opposite the entrance was the stage, with a chamber organ to the side.

Amelia's father had, as usual, reserved seats for them on a second tier bench close to the left-hand side of the stage. Amelia was a pianist, and sitting at that angle to the stage, if there was a piano recital, she was able to get a clear view of the piano keyboard and observe the dexterity of the soloist. She had recently been to a Mozart recital with the acclaimed pianist Mrs Weichsen and was inspired by her exquisite playing on the Broadwood grand piano of the slow first movement of his Sonata in A. Her father had recently purchased a Broadwood for Amelia.

It was advertised as 'quite a new construction, which for delicacy of touch, and beautiful tone, are thought to excel any hitherto invented. Broadwood Piano fortes with a new improvement by which the tone has been rendered remarkably clear and brilliant.' They had laughed at the pompous description, but when it arrived and was placed prominently in the drawing room, Amelia soon discovered the advertisement had lived up to her expectations. It even had six octaves. All the square pianos, which adorned drawing rooms in the city, had five octaves. And it was indeed a grand piano with a perfect, light touch and a beautiful bass tone and Amelia thought that if she practised diligently, she too might give a recital at St Cecilia's Hall.

She loved the concerts, the convivial atmosphere. As did her father who was in the habit of going with the Directors and their friends to Fortune's Tavern after the concert. Her father was keen for her to make a good marriage and as soon as they had set up their house in Queen Street he began taking her to events to meet those people in the higher echelons of society with a view to her marrying well. Amelia was quite aware of this, and perfectly happy to socialise with those of her kind, and the concerts at St Cecilia's Hall were attended by everybody who was anybody in society. And with her father's magnanimous personality he, in no time at all, had made acquaintances with many. So the concerts were a pleasurable event. William would probably be there. He was her brother's best friend. Three years older than her, her brother Malcolm had been living in Edinburgh for many years, training as an advocate under the pupillage of William, a rising star in the legal world, so it was said.

He had become a frequent dinner guest at the house and was a favourite with her father who would expect her to give a recital after dinner on Saturday so she would practise a few hours the next day after her sitting for Henry Raeburn, who was painting her portrait. But this evening, she would settle into her seat and listen to works from one of her favourite composer's – Handel. Amelia had already heard Signora Domenico Corri, and her beautiful, crystal clear, soprano voice so she looked forward to hearing her sing a selection of Handel's Songs and Airs. All in all, it was going to be a very pleasant day, she thought.

VI

John couldn't wait for his day to be over. The heat in the work room made him feel so drowsy but he resisted putting his head down on the bench and nodding off. His typesetting assignments for that day were particularly dull. Advertisements for societies such as the Speculative Society which held meetings in Old College – instituted for improvement in public speaking, membership of that was for privileged people, mostly lawyers, practising their oratory skills for the court room - the Card Assembly and the Pantheon debating Society which John would have liked to have become a member of, but again, only privileged people were welcome.

There was also an advertisement: "*for the Relief of the Destitute Sick who are laid aside by sudden distress, and thereby prevented from following the occupation by which they provide for themselves and families, who have no friends disposed or able to relieve them.*" He couldn't imagine how people's circumstances had become so dire that they were destitute and utterly dependent on the kindness of those who were more fortunate than them. But he had also heard of men, who were not destitute, fraudulently asking for money under the pretence of charity. Still, he surmised, there would always be rogues in any community. And thinking of the community, his thoughts again turned to the riot and, in an attempt to obliterate them, he concentrated furiously on the job in hand hoping James would not bring up the subject again. The shift finally ended and instead of going to the tavern on East Side to meet his friend Peter, a caddie in Edinburgh, he decided to go straight back to his lodgings hoping he would be able to get an early night and some welcome sleep.

"Ye wur late last nicht," Mrs MacFadyen said when he entered the kitchen. "I didnae hear ye come in. Whaur wur ye?"

As he had walked towards his lodgings he had hoped no comment would be made about anything to do with the night before and that dinner would pass uneventfully and he could plead exhaustion because of a late night. He had an honest temperament. He found it difficult to lie and tried his best to appear as nonchalant as possible when he responded. "I wis wi' Peter playing cairds. He kept on winning when we first started, so I had tae redress that an' we didnae notice how late it had become."

Mrs MacFadyen was standing over a wooden board chopping vegetables and with her back to John she asked, "Which tavern were ye at?"

"Matler's on South Bridge,"

"Well ye mist hae heard the rabble."

"Whit rabble?"

"'O' the folk marching tae St Andrew Square, banging drums an' singing. We heard the noise here."

"I maybe did hear something, but we were in the basement so the sound frae the street is muffled."

Mr MacFadyen's heavy footsteps could be heard and he came into the kitchen. He smiled when he saw John, hitching his breeches up over his corpulent body. "Hello son. How ur ye?"

"I wis jist telling John aboot the rabble," said his wife and she recounted the talk of the town.

Now seated at the table and wanting to put a stop to any reminder of the event John adopted a stoical attitude and said, "There's aye gaun tae be people complainin' aboot somethin'

"Aye. That's richt John," retorted Mr MacFadyen.

Mrs MacFadyen glanced at John. "Ye look exhausted. Ye should git an early night."

There was then a commotion outside the door and the MacFadyen children came bursting into the room. John was glad of their arrival as they would distract the conversation away from the event.

"Dougie MacPhail's dad's been arrested," eight-year old Rab blurted out. "He's in the Tolbooth."

Stunned, the mother and father called out in unison, "Whit fur?"

Breathlessly Rab continued, "He wis arrested at the riot last nicht. Sodjers took him and some ithers tae the Magistrate an' he wis pit in prison."

"Oh!" exclaimed Mrs MacFadyen, covering her face with her hands, shocked by the news.

"Aye an'," said Rab is a state of great agitation, "Dougie says he'll be in fur months…"

"Bit," interjected his father, "he's never been in trouble in his life. He's a God fearing man. Whit on earth wis he daein' tae git himsel' arrested?"

"I dinnae ken," Rab replied.

And Lizzie the nine year then said, "wee Jeanie is very upset."

"And so is her Mam," exclaimed three-year old Angus.

"Whisht," Lizzie scolded Angus, "Rab is telling."

In a deeply concerned voice Mrs MacFadyen queried, "How ur they gaun tae survive? Willie is the most popular glover in the city, and Mrs MacPhail couldnae fulfil a' their orders. So, whit will they dae no havin' his money?"

Her husband pondered. "He's been contributing to his Friendly Society. So, they may help oot."

"Maybe."

"It's that bloody Paine…" her husband vehemently responded.

"Dinnae sweer in front o' the bairns."

Furious he replied, "Well. It is. Stirring everybody up wi' his talk aboot equality. Words wilnae feed people. Wages will. Nothin' else. Well …we'll no hae them depend on charity. We'll mak sure they wilnae be destitute."

John immediately recalled the advertisement he had typeset that very day for the Society for the Relief of the Destitute Sick, and he remembered how fortunate he was in not knowing anyone who was in that desperate state.

"How did Mrs MacPhail find oot he wis in prison?" Mrs MacFadyen anxiously asked.

"Dougie said his Mam telt him his Dad had said he wis gaun oot wi' Jimmy an' that he'd be back by ten. Bit he didnae come back. He said she'd hardly slept wi' worrying an' when he still hadnae come hame by seven, she went oot looking fur him thinking maybe he'd been attacked. She spoke tae yin o' the women at the vegetable stalls who telt her folk hud been arrested an' taken tae the Tolbooth."

"She mist hae bin beside hersel' wi' worry," responded his mother.

"She wis," Rab agreed. "Then she plucked up the courage tae gang tae the prison. She gave the Toon Guard his name – Willie MacPhail – an' the man looked at his list. An' there it wis. She telt Dougie she begged the man tae let her see him, bit he wouldnae let her. She wis in a terrible state Dougie said. 'An' the man said he cuid be in prison fir up tae fower months."

"Pair wifie" his mother said, "God kens how they're gaun tae survive"

John sat still at the table, his emotions oscillating between horror and relief. Horror that it could have been him in prison and relief, he desperately hoped, that nobody would discover he had been at the riot.

Practical as ever Mr MacFadyen responded, "We wilnae hae them ending up in the Canongate Charity House. We'll hae tae set up a fund amongst neighbours - they wilnae be able tae git trade tokens. An' we must eat less tae ensure they hae yin guid meal a day. 'An' I'll bake an extra loaf each day we can gie tae them. Noo

Mither, wid ye git the food on the table an' let us eat. Sit doon bairns." Obediently they sat down whilst Mrs MacFadyen handed out the wooden bowls. "We mist be grateful fur whit we hae," said their father sincerely as he sat down at the head of the table. His wife sat opposite with Rab and Lizzie on one side, Angus and John on the other. They all bowed their heads in reverence and put their hands on their laps, as Mr MacFadyen said grace, "Fur whit we are aboot to receive, may the Lord be truly thankit. Amen." They all repeated Amen and sat, unusually, in silence, the children aware that the adults were wrapped up in their own thoughts and would not want to be disturbed. At the end of the meal Mrs MacFadyen announced, "Bed time bairns. Rab and Lizzie ye hae school in the morning an' Angus ye'll be wi' yir mother at the stall. Nae arguments! Be off wi' ye."

When they left the room Mr FacFadyen resumed the conversation about Willie's imprisonment. "I canna believe it. A milder mannered man ye coudnae meet."

John did not contribute. He sat and watched Mrs MacFadyen pick up the wooden bowls and go over to the sink to wipe them with a cloth. She was pondering what her husband had said and finally commented, "Well Mrs MacPhail wis saying o' late that he's become a changed man. He believes whit Paine says. He doesnae think it richt we pay taxes bit they dinnae benefit the people."

"Anyway," her husband retorted, "he shuid be thinking aboot his wife an' family."

"Bit he is."

"No he's no. He's ended up in prison fur a long time an' he'll no be in a position tae feed them. He should hae thocht aboot that afore he got involved in the riot."

"He's a considerate man. Of course he's thinkin' o' his family. That's why he's got involved. He wants their life tae be better. He wants their bairn's lives tae be better."

"Well," her husband responded, "I say leave well alone. Whit aboot you John? Whit do ye hae tae say aboot it?"

"I think we shuid leave well alone."

"See!" Mr MacFadyen indignantly said to his wife, "We're not all like Willie MacPhail, and thank God fur that, fur I wid hate tae think ma wife an' children had difficulty finding money tae feed themselves because I believed in a cause. Bit whit happened, happened an' we must help them as best we can." He raised himself off the chair, retrieved a small leather purse from the pocket of his breeches, went over to his wife and handed her a coin. "Gie that tae Mrs MacPhail an' assure her she'll no go hungry."

"Thank you Tam. Ye're a kind man. I'm lucky tae have ye as mah man." She wiped her hands on her apron and gave him a peck on the cheek.

"It's a sair fecht, is it no," he said to John. Normally an affable man, he became unusually quiet and John took the opportunity to leave, saying he was exhausted from a late night and bade them goodnight.

When John lay down on his bed all he wished was that the nightmare would be over. It had been so difficult for him not to blurt out how he had inadvertently got caught up in the riot and how easy it would have been for him to have been arrested. The soldiers acted brutally and Willie obviously wasn't able to get away quick enough. When they had started to cordon people off he must have got stuck and they would have been given orders to arrest ring leaders and mistakenly thought he was one of them. Well, he would contribute some money towards the MacTaggart family and hopefully that would be an end to the matter. The following morning when he went into the kitchen he felt obliged to ask how Mrs MacPhail was.

"She's been overcome by the kindness o' her neighbours. When I left her she seemed tae be bearing up."

"Is that Dougie's mam ye'r talkin' aboot?" asked Rab, coming into the room. Looking sleepy-eyed, he plonked himself down on his chair at the table. Lizzie followed him, as ever, with wee Angus trailing behind.

"Aye," said his mother. "She's better I'm glad tae say."

"Dae ye think the teacher will mention Dougie's dad?" Rab asked.

His Mother was spooning oatmeal into the bowls when she responded. "I hope no fur his sake." She paused and sat down. "I hope he'll concentrate on the lessons."

"I wonder if a'body else's dad wis arrested?" Rab persisted.

"Hopefully no," his mother responded.

"'An' Jeanie," piped up Lizzie. "I hope she won't cry today. It wis awfy upsetting seein' her greetin' yesterday."

"I ken. Bit dinnae worry. They'll be all richt. Noo, jist eat up an' git awa tae school."

"I'm awa tae," said John getting off his chair. "I'll see ye at denner time." And he left.

There were no soldiers visible on his way to work and he started to think life would indeed return to normal. However, to his dismay, his first assignment at work was a notice from the Lord Provost and Magistrates. A meeting had been held the previous evening at the Merchants Hall:

"Resolved Unanimously: That this company collectively and individually will give every aid in their power towards carrying into effect and measures that have been adopted by the Lord Provost and Magistrates, and the Sheriff of the county, for checking and suppressing the disturbances that which the city is threatened.

Resolved Unanimously: That the thanks of this company are transmitted to the Lord Provost and Magistrates to the Sheriff of the county and to the Commander-in-Chief and the other military officers for the temperate and spirited measure they have taken in endeavouring to repress the riots that have lately happened.

Resolved Unanimously: That this company subscribe FIFTY GUINEAS to be given as a reward for the discovery of the leaders and instigators of the late disturbances, or of the writers of the incendiary letters or seditious advertisements which have lately appeared."

God almighty, John thought. Fifty guineas. That is a fortune. His hands started to shake thinking his fate could be the same as Willie's but he had to compose himself in case James noticed his agitation so discreetly began to breathe deeply to quieten his emotions so he could concentrate on the job in hand.

"I read the notice," said James. "That's a lot o' money! I wish I hud some information an' cuid git that reward."

"Um," responded John. "It is a fair lot o' money." And ignoring James, he continued to pick up his type letters but at a more frantic pace.

Amelia, on the other hand, had a pleasant morning. She had another sitting with Henry Raeburn who was painting her portrait in their drawing room and so had reminded Meg to put her hair in the same style as the previous Friday. Remaining in the same position, not moving any of her facial muscles was a challenge for Amelia. She thought Raeburn looked so serious, she often wanted to burst out laughing but had to contain her mirth lest he be offended. Then in the afternoon, she would practise the Mozart.

VII

"I thought we'd see you at the concert on Thursday," Lord Hugh addressed William as they sat round the dining table.

"Well sir," William responded, adjusting his napkin on his lap. "I was rather caught up in the arrests of men involved in the riot last Wednesday evening." He turned in the direction of Lord Hugh who was seated at the head of the dining table.

"Yes," Lord Hugh responded, "it was the talk of the club when I went the following morning. I heard two guns being fired from the castle and thought it must be a celebration of some sort.

"Yes Father," Amelia enthusiastically agreed. "I heard them as well and presumed they were extending the King's Birthday celebrations."

"Quite the reverse," responded William in a stern voice addressing Amelia sitting opposite. "The guns were fired to call up the military from Leith to quell the bunch of seditious rebellers intent on causing destruction to the Government."

"What were they protesting about?" asked Amelia innocently.

"I don't want to trouble you with the details…"

"But I'd like to know."

Sitting next to William, Malcolm piped up, "It was the talk in chambers."

"Indeed it was," William replied to Malcolm sitting on his right, and popped another oyster into his mouth.

"I think it is important Amelia should know about these things," Lord Hugh rejoined, "but at the club nobody seemed to know the specific reason."

"Well," said William authoritatively, "it was a bunch of rebellers wanting voting reform, which of course is ridiculous, and will get them nowhere." He paused. "But smashing the windows of the Lord Provost's house in St Andrew Square, terrifying the living daylights out of him and his family, will certainly get them into prison."

"I also think," said Malcolm, "it could have been to do with the slave trade, and Dundas' attitude. Many people were upset about him wanting to delay the abolition of it."

"The slave trade?" queried Amelia.

I'll tell you in a minute Amelia," said Malcolm. "These are two important issues. And Dundas has aggrieved many over them. Firstly, he has rejected Sheridan's motion for voting reform on several occasions, over several years. And secondly, there has been condemnation of him postponing the abolition of the slavery bill. When Wilberforce introduced the motion for immediate abolition of the slave trade in the House of Commons, Dundas retorted by saying let's do it in stages…"

"I personally think it should be done in stages," William interjected.

"That is no excuse," Lord Hugh indignantly retorted. "Wilberforce is right. I think we should abolish the abominable slave trade forthwith."

"I want to know more about it," said Amelia.

"I don't think it's anything you should worry your pretty little head about Amelia," responded William. "You've got other things to think about. Your painting, playing the piano." He smiled at her. "You should stick to those pursuits and not bother about the world of men."

"How condescending William," laughed Lord Hugh. "She's more intelligent than you think you know."

"And I do want to know."

"It's a trade where merchants make a lot of money. Don't you agree Lord Hugh?" replied William. "You must have some interests involved in the slave trade."

"No, I don't," Lord Hugh adamantly responded. "I personally don't approve of it."

"But even if you're not personally involved," William remarked sycophantically, "you must see the fiscal benefits. It's helping the economy enormously. All that wealth coming in. Trade and the like."

"Yes I do see that," Lord Hugh agreed. "But I would rather we benefitted from different pursuits."

"And who are the slaves father?"

"Black men and women," stated Malcolm.

"You don't have to go into it in detail Malcolm," said his father.

"I think it is important Amelia gets this education father,"

"But Amelia doesn't want to hear about this Malcolm," William haughtily retorted.

"Yes I do."

"Well," Malcolm resumed, "when Britain colonised the West Indies we transported – and still do - thousands of black men and women from Africa to work on the sugar plantations there. Do you know, forty-two thousand Africans were transported to the West Indies last year, it's disgraceful. And the conditions on board the slave boats are dreadful. Just recently I read that thousands die during the journey."

"Yes. I hear what you're saying Malcolm and I understand your ethics," said William deciding it was auspicious to be less dogmatic, "but I agree with Dundas who, quite rightly, said in the House the other day that if Britain wasn't involved some other foreign power would take over the slave trade. I don't see how it can be stopped when so much money is being gained from it. It's good for the economy. And its profits that motivate those in power."

"But it's not right treating people so abominably. They have a right to dignity just as much as we do."

"They get fed and watered Malcolm," scoffed William. "After all, they should be glad somebody is looking after them."

Malcolm, his anger rising retorted, "Yes. But the conditions they are being kept in…."

"Yes. I've also read reports," said his father.

"But again," William interjected, "I think Dundas is right. If it wasn't Britain involved in the slave trade, it would be another power."

"Perhaps," Malcolm conceded. "But I don't approve of it. And the conditions they're kept in …"

"What conditions?" asked Amelia.

"I've read they get beaten. Are kept in appalling conditions. They're treated dreadfully."

"It's unlike you to be so vocal Malcolm," smirked William.

"Maybe I've been in disguise all the years you've known me."

Realising his stance was perhaps too harsh, William decided to temper his opinions. "That may be so, but the economy is the most important thing of all."

"Not if it's at the cost of human beings, "Amelia responded sympathetically. "That's not right."

"There are many things in life," said William in an authoritative voice, "that are not right. But good for the system."

Benjamin, the butler, started to serve the venison and fresh vegetables from the market garden at Lord Hugh's estate, and the conversation resumed. William, as usual, dominated.

"Anyway," William continued, "back to the riot. Robert told me …"

"Yes," said Lord Hugh. "I heard about them terrorising Dundas's mother at her house in George Square two days before. That was dreadful. Unwarranted violence."

"Indeed it was. Dundas' nephew Frances was dining with his brother and he looked out of Robert's drawing room window and noticed a crowd carrying an image suspended between two poles. Apparently it was Dundas. He went to his mother's house nearby. She was in the drawing room with Admiral Duncan. The crowd were shouting and cheering and a piece of wood was thrown up against the window, followed by jeering and throwing of missiles."

"It was quite a spectacle apparently," said Lord Hugh. "Frances came to the club the following morning."

"Well," William continued, "as the mob persisted in jeering and throwing missiles, Francis and Admiral Duncan came out of the house. Admiral Duncan was brandishing Lady Arniston's crutch but he was seized and beaten with his own weapon and he quickly went back in to the house. Then Sheriff Pringle arrived, followed shortly by soldiers, and read out the Riot Act. Apparently two shots were fired, but nobody was injured. The crowd dispersed but some time later returned to George Square, and the ranks had swelled. It was a terrific crowd Robert told us and they started to fling missiles at his windows. It was terrifying he said."

"It was disgraceful," Lord Hugh responded after hearing the tale. "And vandalising the Lord Provost's house. Disgraceful behaviour."

"Oh," remarked William "that's what these rebellers are like. Violent people. All stirred up by that scoundrel Paine."

"Yes I've seen pamphlets around town with quotations from Thomas Paine's book," said Amelia.

"Well," responded Malcolm, "it's reckoned Dundas has interests in thirty-four out of the forty-five constituencies."

"Dundas," William replied, "is keen to get the best representation in Parliament."

"But," Malcolm responded, "for whose benefit?"

"The country of course."

"Setting soldiers onto rioters is hardly to the benefit of anyone. Issues are best resolved without resorting to violence," Malcolm retorted.

"I agree with you Malcolm. Of course violence is to be abhorred, but when you have a mob acting in a malicious manner, how else can they be contained except by force. Persuasion wouldn't work when passions are running high, but force does. It immediately quells the riotous atmosphere and acts as a warning that such behaviour will not be tolerated." He paused then said firmly. "They are acting illegally and should be punished by the courts. Dissenters are dangerous, irrational. These passions have to be dealt with harshly."

"But according to reports," Lord Hugh countered, "the rioters were not armed. And I think the decision to send in troops was inauspicious. A provocative move because inevitably that would enflame the anger and discontent I am led to believe many people feel. The force was disproportionate."

"Yes," William replied. "There is merit in that it could be concluded it was disproportionate but in reality what else could have been done? They were hell bent sir on causing chaos, and if they hadn't been stopped in that path, God knows what other destruction they could have caused."

"Yes, I suppose you're right," Lord Hugh conceded after deliberating for a moment.

"But surely you can understand their anger," responded Malcolm. "Rumour has it there's bribery and corruption involved in the voting system in all the burghs."

"I shouldn't believe everything you hear," William re-joined. "And the rumour isn't founded on fact."

"Yes it is," Malcolm retorted. "The last petition Sheridan presented at the House in April was signed by nine thousand Burgesses – from fifty of the sixty-six Royal Burghs – and they outlined evidence of the abuses in the Burghs. Dundas, of course…"

William immediately interjected, "Dundas is a good Home Secretary. He is only doing what he thinks is best for the country. But if there is evidence that bribery and corruption are indeed involved in the voting system then it could be dealt with in the courts."

"No it couldn't," Malcolm vehemently countered. "Magistrates are self-elected. There's no judicature in Scotland who can hold them to account. You must surely know that William?"

"Yes," William conceded. "I suppose that's right".

"Well that is what these nine thousand Burgesses are complaining about. They want parliament to set up a Bill of Regulations to redress the mismanagement, misapplication of money and many other grievances that the self-elected Magistrates have been involved with since time immemorial …"

"But what they're proposing," William immediately intervened, "is to uproot the constitution which has been in place for four hundred years."

"And why not?" Malcolm's voice raised in passion. "Because," he hastily added before William intervened again. "Fair representation should be an integral part of democracy. As Aristotle said: 'Democracy is when the indigent, and not men of property, are the rulers.' "

"That was two thousand years ago," William scoffed. "Times move on. Change."

"No they don't," Malcolm angrily responded. "Why do you think there was a riot in St Andrew Square? There is much anger towards Dundas for denying there are any abuses in the Burghs. Of course he'd say that. It's in his vested interests to keep the status quo. The councils and the Magistrates are his puppets. And," continued Malcolm getting into his stride "it's not just working-class people who are involved in the reform movement, many nobles are taking up the cause. The Earl of Buchan for instance, Henry Erskine's brother, is a vocal supporter of reform."

William ignored his comments, "It is of great concern to the establishment and these revolts about reform are causing great concern to Dundas, and his peers because they think it could lead to anarchy …

"The only way it could lead to anarchy," interjected Malcolm," is if Dundas should treat these grievances with contempt. That would indeed be a foolish act on his part because the populace would no longer trust those in Parliament."

"Our constitution is the best and most admired in the world," William firmly added.

"Then why," said Malcolm getting agitated, "have established peers such as Charles Grey and other people rooted in the establishment, formed a society for the purposes of restoring freedom of election and a more equal representation of the people in England who also have petitioned for reform."

"They're misguided," responded William.

"Of course they're not misguided! You have to take your blinkers off William and truly appreciate what many people in North and South Britain are seeking. And Sheridan in the House told Dundas that if he doesn't pay attention to the grievances then his popularity in Scotland will cease to exist. He can't assume favouritism when abuses can readily be seen so why is he not doing anything about it? Because it's in his best interest to maintain control of all elections in Scotland and I think it's a foolish move for him to ignore the unrest."

"But I can understand why he is taking his stance. Of course he doesn't want masses causing chaos around the country."

"As I said," Malcolm replied, "anarchy will only erupt if the voices of the people are not heard."

Lord Hugh had been listening attentively to their arguments and finally made a comment. "I think it commendable people have the courage to speak their minds. I personally approve of universal suffrage. I don't approve of tenants being subjugated to the whims of their landlords. I've always believed in a fair system."

"Yes father," said Amelia, "and that's why you are much loved."

"That's a truly commendable opinion sir," said William, "but most landowners act in the best interests of their tenants."

"Not necessarily," retorted Malcolm.

"Oh they do," replied William authoritatively. "I mean …"

"Well obviously a large faction of society does not agree with you William," responded Amelia.

"Maybe not," William conceded.

"But why resort to violence?" Lord Hugh asked.

"Because their voices aren't being heard father. Surely that's the only reason people resort to violence."

"Not necessarily," responded William. "Some people have a violent nature. We know that from the cases we hear in court. Some people do have violent tendencies."

"But not women and children."

"Oh we do have lads up in court Amelia," said William.

"We had a lad the other day who was violent. He knocked a landlady down after he'd stolen cheese from her shop."

"What happened to him?" Amelia asked in a concerned voice.

"Stripped to the waist, and given fifty lashes on his back."

"That's sounds unnecessarily brutal."

"Well. I don't think he'll be stealing anything again. But … back to the riot…"

"Hopefully the atmosphere will quieten down" said Lord Hugh.

"Let's hope so sir. Excuse me, I've just remembered," William turned his head towards Malcolm. "There's the trial of John Taylor coming up in the High Court on the twelfth of July. Robert Dundas will be for the crown. I think it would be a good experience for you to attend."

"Who's John Taylor?" Amelia enquired.

"Allegedly one of the ringleaders of the riot at St Andrew Square. The evidence against him is strong, and of course Robert will create a persuasive case in court."

"Who's defending?" asked Malcolm.

"Adam Gillies and Charles Ross. But, it's a fait accompli. He will be found guilty."

"Why is that?" asked Amelia.

"Because Robert is an exceptionally talented advocate. It is rare for him to lose a case." He paused, "You've become very vocal Amelia."

"Yes," said Lord Hugh. "She's a spirited woman." He smiled at her. "Just like my beloved wife, whom I still miss after all these years."

There was a pause in the conversation as each digested Lord Hugh's sentiments. Then William asked, "Are you going back to the estate for the summer?"

"Indeed we are William. And I think it fair to say that Amelia and I are very much looking forward to it."

"Yes," agreed Amelia. "A welcome respite from city life."

"I tell you what I think would be a welcome respite from life right now and that is if you would please play the piano Amelia."

"What a good idea William," Lord Hugh replied. "Would you do us the honour of playing some music my dear? That would rest our intellects." He smiled at William and Malcolm.

"Yes father," and she imparted a loving look at him

Looking contented Lord Hugh said, "So let us retire to the drawing room and be serenaded by Amelia. And Benjamin, could you please bring in the port?"

"Of course sir."

VIII

When William jauntily left the house he started to contemplate the evening. How lovely Amelia looked he thought. And such a spirited girl. He liked that in a woman. He hadn't paid much attention to her when she had arrived in the city, she was just his friend's sister, but this evening was the first time he had noticed what an attractive woman she was becoming. She looked particularly elegant with her beige brocaded dress exposing her slender neck. And she looked so poised when she was playing the piano. Maybe he should start thinking of her in a romantic light, although he knew his career took priority over everything. He aspired to be a judge on the bench of the High Court of Justiciary and if Malcolm was wise, he should quell his libertarian ideas if he wanted to march up the legal ladder. Dundas's views pervaded the courts and with his nephew Lord Advocate his ideals were sure to be advanced. No, it wouldn't be in Malcolm's best interests to make his views known in chambers. He'd have to work on him. Get him to see reason. Dundas's opinions were authoritatively persuasive and would ultimately prevail so it would be foolish of Malcolm to jeopardise his future career by siding with rebellers notions. Yes, he would work on him and with that decision made he quickened his pace and marched back to his digs.

How dapper William looked, Amelia thought as she retired that evening. He really was rather handsome, if not a rather opinionated man. Although marriage was the last thing she was thinking about, she did wonder if he would make a good suitor. Certainly her father liked and respected him. And Malcolm thought very highly of him. Gosh, Malcolm was quite forthright this evening. He usually pandered to William's opinions but it would be good if he developed a mind of his own rather than being influenced by William's sentiments. She enjoyed the discussion and despite William dismissively saying it was 'man's matters' she decided she would take a greater interest in politics and read the papers when they went to the estate. And maybe she could ask Charlotte to stay with them for a while. Her father would probably be glad if she had a companion for some of the time. Yes, she would ask her next week at the last art class of the term

When Lord Hugh retired, he immediately started to think of his wife. His beloved Margaret who had died giving birth to Amelia. Distraught with despair, afterwards he agonised what else he could have done to save the life of his beloved. He had engaged the services of the most competent doctor in the parish. He trusted his judgement implicitly but she had haemorrhaged after the birth and he could do nothing but watch the life of his beloved ebb away. The doctor had tried everything to stem the flow of blood but to no avail, and before she passed away in his arms she said to him, in a voice barely audible, "Promise me you will look after the baby. And Hugh, I know I shall always be in your heart." He held her tenderly till her last breath. And the baby? He couldn't have cared less about the 'healthy child' as the doctor pronounced. He didn't want a healthy child, he wanted a healthy wife. She was so full of vigour. Their marriage had not been one of convenience, they had had a deep love for one another, and he knew she could never be replaced.

Hours after her death, and the grief had started to subside, he realised he had to take charge of all the practicalities. Malcolm, their three-year old, would at least have the comfort of nanny's company, and he would employ a nursemaid for the wailing baby, whom he blamed for causing the death of the only woman he had ever loved. But he had no choice but to continue organising the estate, looking after the tenants who depended on him. He had to keep going on, despite his grief-stricken state. He knew he couldn't commit suicide, he had made a promise to her to look after the children, but his will to live had gone. Although he made a point of going to the nursery at the same time every day to make a herculean effort to feel something towards the tiny thing. And every time he saw Amelia he remembered his beloved's dying words and would pick the baby up to give her a cuddle, at least make an effort. And Malcom appeared to cope with the loss of his mother. He was a strong boy, stubborn but with a kind nature, like himself as a young man.

In his early teenage years, he would ride out with his own father surveying the estate. His father was well respected by his tenants for he was a fair man, making sure they were never without and at Christmas he would present each family with a slaughtered pig to sustain them over the harsh winter months. And all the tenants were given a strip of land with which to cultivate vegetables. He created a good community. When Hugh was sixteen he went to Edinburgh to study law. It was a wrench leaving his family, but he adjusted and blended in with the social life. That's where he had met Margaret - at a Caledonian Hunt Ball.

He was reserved by nature and when he first set eyes on her he thought she was the most beautiful woman he had ever seen with such an infectious laugh. They developed an instant friendship and that was all he contemplated. He was then seventeen, and focused on developing a career at the bar, but, as the months progressed, they regularly met one another at the society balls. His personality started to blossom on each occasion they met and within a short time he realised, to his utter surprise, he had fallen madly in love with her. In love with her laugh, her energy, her joie de vivre, far removed from her father, an austere character. A judge, he had the reputation of being harsh on the bench, but she was like a ray of sunshine and he couldn't stop thinking about her: writing his briefs during the day; in court; in the evenings with friends and when he retired to bed. He became consumed with a passion, which the more he tried to quell, the worse it became. And so he finally succumbed to the realisation she was the love of his life and he would ask her to marry him.

Then tragedy struck. His father died in a hunting accident whilst they were giving chase. His horse had stumbled over a ditch and his father had been thrown and hit his head with a terrific blow on a tree. He died soon after, and Hugh was recalled home to take over the estate at the age of eighteen.

He agonised as to what he could do about Margaret because he knew inevitably he would have to become ensconced in the daily goings on of the estate and wouldn't have the opportunity of going back to Edinburgh, and the thought of losing her caused him untold pain. He made a decision. He would ask her to marry him. Neither of them had wanted to be married so young but he hoped, with all his heart, she would not refuse.

It was a balmy summers evening when they had met at another ball and immediately the interval was announced he asked her to step outside. She laughed, "What plans are you up to Hugh? I hope you're not scheming something."

"No indeed not. Please accompany me outside. There is something I want to ask you." He saw her heart beat underneath her gown and hoped he hadn't misread her feelings. But he had to risk it. She took his arm and as they stood outside he got down on one knee and asked, "Will you marry me?"

"Oh don't be so silly Hugh. Get up. Of course I will. Did you ever doubt it?

"Not really dearest." he said, smiling affectionately at her.

He was apprehensive about asking her father for her hand but the estate was flourishing and his father had given him a good training in management and he knew he could offer her a comfortable existence, albeit away from the social life in Edinburgh, but she had already said she didn't mind in the slightest abandoning balls and the accoutrements attached to Edinburgh society life. She assured him she would be happy to just be in his company. Her father did agree to the marriage and they wed in the chapel on the estate. He had asked the tenants to attend so they felt part of the ceremony, party to their heavenly union.

Sadly, though, his mother did not attend the ceremony. She had become a recluse since the shock of her husband's sudden death and never ventured forth from that room. He thought she would be delighted when told of Margaret's pregnancy but even that, and the subsequent birth of Malcolm did not alleviate her catatonic state and she passed away soon after he was born. Margaret had already taken over as mistress of the house. Liked by all, her diplomatic skills and easy charm won everybody over – and then tragically she unexpectedly died. But now, all those years later, he saw his beloved's nature reflected in Amelia and, over time, he had begun to love his daughter as a father should.

IX

The next day was the Sabbath. A day when the predominantly Presbyterian city of Edinburgh obeyed the rules of the kirk that 'all must rest from workaday labours, words and thoughts and spend the whole time in public and private worship and other holy ways.'

Over breakfast, John and the family discussed the dilemma Mrs MacPhail felt about going to church. "She hadnae been keen tae tak' the family tae the service," said Mrs MacFadyen, "bit she knew she wud be castigated by one of' yon elders if she didnae go. But she also knew Reverend Fletcher would allude tae the fact some o' his parishioners hae been arrested. So," she continued "she's full o' trepidation."

"Aye. She will be," her husband stoically added.

"Well," responded his wife, adopting her matriarchal stance, "we'll walk tae church thegither." She directed her attention to Rab: "After we've finished gang and tell them we'll be waiting fur them in the street. 'An' they're tae join us after church tae share oor food."

As they walked to the Tolbooth Parish kirk at the top of the High Street, all dressed in their Sunday best, they passed groups of the city's elite animatedly chatting as they entered the High Kirk and John thought what a sombre contrast their group presented.

When they arrived at church they went to their allotted pews. As usual, it was a full congregation. Reverend Fletcher began the service inviting the congregation to join him in saying the Lord's Prayer. Everyone stood with their heads bowed and began to slowly recite the prayer. 'Our Father which art in heaven, hallowed be your name. Your kingdom come, your will be done, on earth as it is in heaven. Give us this day our daily bread, and forgive us our debts, as we also have forgiven our debtors. And lead us not into temptation, but deliver us from evil. For thine is the kingdom, the power, and the glory for ever, Amen.' With much shuffling and clatter the congregation sat down and awaited the deliverance of Reverend Fletcher's sermon.

He stepped up to the pulpit. A silence descended on the congregation as all eyes were directed on him when he ponderously began. "And lead us not into temptation, but deliver us from evil." He paused. "Temptation is a sin against God who is our master. Our master not just on this Sabbath day, but every day of the week. And it is a sin to transgress against the laws of our God. And it is a sin to transgress against the laws of the land we dwelleth in. A sin to disobey those laws." He stopped speaking and for several minutes and pointedly glared at specific members of the congregation – including Mrs MacPhail.

He regained his composure and continued. "A sin to disobey these laws" he reiterated, then got into his stride. "By disobeying the laws and committing violent acts, these members of our congregation incur the wrath of the Lord. And that is indeed a sin." The last word was delivered with full force to enable the congregation to dwell on the significance and ramifications of the word. "Romans 13. 'But if thou do that which is evil," he paused, then vehemently said, "be afraid; for he beareth not the sword in vain: for he is the minister of God, a revenger to execute wrath upon him that doeth evil.' And it was an evil," he paused, "wilful act on those members of our congregation who endangered the life of the Lord Provost. A respected man in our community who is responsible for law and order." Again he stopped and targeted his gaze on the perpetrators relatives. "The perpetrators of this wilful act should seek the Lord's guidance. Romans 13, 'whosoever therefore resisteth the power of the Lord', resisteth the ordinance of God; and they that resist shall receive to themselves damnation." The last word reverberated around the walls of the church and everyone in the congregation sat mute. "And damnation is a terrible state to contemplate."

He paused to enable his flock to contemplate this terrible state. He then resumed. "Those who are damned in the eyes of our Lord shall be sent to hell. To rot amongst all the other sinners in that hellish furnace of fire. And for committing a violent act those perpetrators will indeed be condemned to rot in hell, for that is what they deserve. No salvation for them unless," he paused, "they choose to seek the path of hallowed redemption. Redemption is the only path to avoid the gates of hell. These sinners must make penance to our Lord for their heinous transgressions. To redeem their souls back into our flock, they must earnestly pray, and seek guidance from our Lord to avoid entering the gates of hell. And the gates of hell are a terrible place. A place where the soul can never find rest. Never find peace. The only state is one of perpetual torment. And a tormented soul is a terrible place for any member of our flock to behold. A soul in constant turmoil. What a thought brethren! What a thought." Standing as rigid as a rock in the pulpit he paused for several minutes. "These perpetrators in our congregation who committed evil acts will be committed to the furnace of hell … unless … they can redeem themselves in the eyes of the Lord. Now, that is some considerable task to behold. How can perpetrators of evil, possibly redeem themselves to the Lord? I tell you," he raised his voice in emphasis, "by prayers. By praying long and hard, to seek forgiveness for their transgressions. That is the path to avoid the gates of hell. They must pray fervently, from the depths of their soul – if they still have a conscience – and if they still have a conscience, and if they do that, there may be a possibility they will be redeemed from that hellish place. We must all pray to help these lost souls, and hope that the black pit they have fallen into will, with our prayers, soon be shrouded in light to bring them back into the arms of our Lord.

Trust in our Lord, and all will be well. Keep faith in our Lord, and all will be well. If we do not have trust and faith, then we are condemned for ever. Condemned for ever. And condemnation is as hellish a state as damnation. And may we all be retrieved from that through our love for our God. Praying for redemption for the sinners amongst us is what I ask my flock to do. And may these sinners never commit another violent act. May they always obey the laws of God and the laws of the land. May they seek penance at the very feet of the Lord. If they do not fervently seek penance at the feet of the Lord, then there is no doubt – no doubt at all – that they will be condemned to the gates of hell. No funeral for them. No prayers for them. No redemption for them." A lengthy pause as he glowered at several of his parishioners. "No redemption for them." He eventually lowered his eyes and pronounced, "Here endeth the sermon. Praise to the Lord. Amen," A subdued congregation voiced "Amen" in unison.

After the service the congregation deposited what spare pennies they could into the beggar's bowl, as was the tradition, and silently left the church.. On the steps outside, Mrs MacTaggart's youngest daughter Maggie clutched her mother's hand, looked earnestly into her eyes and anxiously asked, "Will Pa go tae the gates o' hell Ma."

"Of course not," her mother hastily responded. "He's a guid man. He wis daein' whit he thought wis right."

"Bit," Maggie persisted, "he's in prison. He cannae hae dain whit is richt."

Camouflaging her true feelings Mrs MacPhail reassuringly responded saying, "He'll be back soon. Noo gang 'n' tak' hauns with Lizzie 'n' walk quietly doon the road."

John, overhearing the comments, mused on how different Hugh Blair's sermon would have been at the High Kirk in St Giles. Renowned as a libertarian and philosopher, John felt sure his stance on the rebellers would have been more sympathetic, less dogmatically antagonistic towards his parishioners. And he thought Willie, like him, had inadvertently got caught up in the atmosphere.

"I wish the Minister hadnae been sae harsh," Mrs MacFadyen said to her neighbour as they walked alongside one another back to their tenement.

"It's only whit I expected," Mrs MacPhail responded in a resigned voice.

"He can be unforgiving at times," said Mr MacFadyen. "It's his way, but ye mustn't tak' it tae much tae heart. Ye hae tae remain strong an' hope Willie doesn't git sent fur trial, bit jist receives a short prison sentence."

"That's ma hope," responded the poor woman. "Bit I ken Maggie weel enough. She'll be persistent in asking me aboot her Pa gaun tae hell."

"Ye just hae tae reassure her that he's a guid man, an' that he'll be hame soon," Mrs MacFadyen told her.

"That's ma firm belief, an' we can put this a' behind us an' git on as afore. But I dinnae ken whit'll happen at school. The children who were at the church this morning will, I'm sure, be wanting tae talk aboot it th'morn."

"Well there's nothing ye can dae aboot that," Mrs MacFadyen firmly responded. "Ye hae tae hope the children are strong enough tae tak the comments. An' school will soon be ower, the term finishes in a few weeks. Willie will be hame by then, please God, an' all will be well."

"The first trial is on the twelfth of July," Mr MacFadyen said in a sombre tone. "We'll hae tae see whit the judges an' jury decide. Certainly Dundas will be keen fur his nephew tae find the man guilty."

"Dae ye ken whae it is?" John asked.

"It's John Taylor. He's been charged as being the ringleader o' the St Andrew Square riot."

"There's nae point in surmising whit will happen," said John. "Jist tak each day as it comes."

"Aye. That's the only way," responded Mrs MacPhail. "An' we are so grateful fur yer support. A' the neighbours support. We'll pull through."

"O' course ye will," assured Mrs MacFadyen giving her friend a comforting hug. "An' let's hope Reverend Fletcher's sermon this evening is less harsh."

"Could I say the children huv come doon wi' something?"

"Naw. Ye canny dae that," Mrs MacFadyen's emphatically responded. "Yer absence wid be noticed. In fact, the Minister cuid even comment on that. Ye hae tae be strang. Haud yer heid up high. Keep on reminding yoursel' whit a guid man Willie is an' try an' close yer lugs tae the Minister's comments. An' tell the bairns tae dae the same."

"Is there ony news frae the prison?" asked Mr MacFadyen.

"Naw. I'm no allowed tae see him. I dinnae ken whit's gaun tae happen."

"Weel, gang tae th' prison next week 'n' ask agin if ye can see him."

"Aye" Mrs PacPhail meekly responded. "I'll dae that."

"An' start praying he'll soon be released" added Mrs MacFadyen.

"Aye. That's a' we can dae," emphasised her husband.

X

The trial, John realised, would be reported when he was still on his annual visit to his parents. And when he boarded the mail coach at Ramsay's Inn, at the foot of St Mary's Wynd, he started to ruminate on when he left his home to start his apprenticeship. His father had told him when he boarded the coach for Edinburgh, "Ye're a man noo. Be strong." Certainly his voice had broken, he had started to get a growth of hair on his chin, but it required a huge effort on his part to suppress the aching feel of loneliness on that first coach journey to the city. Three gentlemen were also in the coach so he wasn't going to make a fool of himself and cry. His father had told him 'be strong' and that was the stance he adopted all those years ago when he went to live with an unfamiliar family, and work for people he had never met. Fortunately, all had worked out. And with the improved postal service he was able to keep in touch with his parents, and they with him.

The coach arrived early evening and John had already written to say he didn't need to be met, as they had done before, he would enjoy the stroll back walking the familiar route he used to take to school. He did fleetingly wish he was young and carefree again but the moment passed and he looked forward to seeing his parents. When he approached the house he could hear them discussing their day, as they always did. He opened the door with a flourish. His mother heard the latch, turned and beamed at him when he entered. They were standing by the stove and she immediately went to him and gave him a welcome embrace.

"Great tae see ye son. It's been a long time."

"Indeed it has. An' I'm awy pleased tae be back. An' whit's that delicious smell?"

"It's yer favourite. Salmon," she smiled.

"Hello son," said his father coming towards him with an outstretched hand. "How are ye?"

"Fine," responded John, firmly shaking his hand.

"An' the journey?"

"It's always a pleasure tae git oot o' the city."

"Well, it's a pleasure tae hae ye back fur the week. Come," he led him by his arm to the table. "Let's eat. Ye must be hungry."

"I am indeed. An' how good it is tae see ye both well, an' I'm thinkin' happy."

"Aye," his mother said as she started to spoon the food onto plates. "We've always felt guid in yin anither's company."

"Sae, how is life in the city?" his father asked as he settled in his chair.

"Guid," John responded as his mother laid a plate before him.

"Sit down Ma. Let's say grace an' then we'll hear the news." Once done his father asked. "How are the MacFadyen family?"

"They're well. The bairns are getting older but they're still as boisterous. They're guid people tae lodge wi'." He contemplated a moment then added. "I'm fortunate." and, addressing his mother, he said, "This is delicious Ma. Thank ye"

She smiled. "I've always loved cooking fur ye John. An' I thought as salmon is yer favourite food, that'll be his first denner back hame."

"Very thoughtful. As ever."

"Noo," his father said, adopting a stern expression. "We read aboot the riots."

"It's quietened down noo," John replied.

"We were worried aboot ye,"

"Ye needn't hae been. I'm fine."

"Wis it no dangerous wi' people rampaging aroond the toun?"

"No. I felt perfectly safe," he lied, thinking of the soldiers hanging around North Bridge.

"But we read aboot folk smashing windaes in pairts o' the city."

"Aye. It was George Square an' St Andrew Square. It was a while ago. Things hae returned tae normal."

"I dinnae think that will last," his father said forcibly. "When I wis in the tavern the other nicht, men there were saying they were gaun tae be setting up a Friends o' the People society in Penicuik mill."

Aghast, John responded: "In Penicuik?"

"Aye. An' according tae them, lots o' societies are gaun tae be set up roond the country. It's a movement. An' I dinnae think it's gaun tae be quelled."

"But ye're no thinking aboot getting involved are ye?"

"No. I'll probably no," his father reassured him.

"Oh I hope ye dinnae," his mother said her voice suffused with anxiety.

"Well," her husband responded. "Lord Hugh is a fair landlord. I dinnae think the tenants on this estate hae grievances. Bit frae whit I've heard he's unusual. Ither landlords around here couldnae care less aboot the needs o' their tenants 'n' that's why they want tae be able tae vote people into the Toun Councils an' Government who will be on their side. Hae ye read Paine's book?" he asked John.

"No I huvnae." John was beginning to feel uncomfortable with the conversation.

"Bit workin' on the newspaper, ye mist at least hae read his quotes."

"Aye. I huv. Obviously I've typeset some o' them bit I dinnae want tae git involved."

"Well," his father retorted, "I've got a copy o' the Rights of Man."

Surprised John asked, "How did ye manage that wi' the King banning the distribution?"

"Och. They're everywhere. A guy was hawking them in the tavern. He said he couldnae sell enough of them. He said instead o' reading Bunyan's Pilgrims Progress, they're reading Paine's Rights of Man." He chortled.

"Did naebody complain aboot him selling them?"

"Quite the reverse," said his father. "Jist aboot every man there was purchasing a copy. Has nobody been selling them in the taverns ye gang tae in Edinburgh?"

"No. They wouldnae risk it. The Magistrates' eyes an' ears are everywhere in the city. It wid be too dangerous tae sell them there. They wid ken they wid be arrested."

"Well according tae the man I git the book frae, they're being sold everywhere in Scotland." He chuckled. "He said it's even been translated into gaelic."

"Guid heavens" John remarked. "I huvnae heard anything aboot that in Edinburgh. Mind ye, there's a trial coming at the end o' the week. A man called John Taylor. He's charged wi' being the ringleader o' the riot at St Andrew Square. I shuid think folk are nervous aboot even mentioning Paine's book when the officials are doing all they can tae quell ony interest there might be in it."

They sat eating for a moment in silence, then his father recommenced, "I can see why the Government are worried aboot a revolution here. Paine's words are provocative. He's obviously in favour o' the tidal wave agin the aristocracy in France an' giein' power tae the people." He paused. "I dinnae think the country hae seen the end o' the unrest." He resumed eating, then continued. "I wis reading it agin last nicht. Paine makes some very provocative statements. Let me see if I can mind ony." He contemplated for a moment. "Aye. Here's a quote: 'A Government where the executive and legislative power meet in a single person, hae no more pretence to freedom: it is perfect despotism: and the people who submit tae it are in a state of slavery.' That is a very strong statement."

"Indeed it is," agreed John.

"An' despotism is the word the French National Assembly used tae rouse the masses tae revolt, accusing the controlling powers as being despotic."

"Aye, bit's different here," John quickly responded

"How?" his father immediately retorted. "We have – an' I'll quote again – a government where the executive an' legislative power meet in a single person. An' according tae Paine that constitutes 'perfect despotism'."

"Well," said John getting heated "We may well hae a government that cuid be called despotic bit there the similarities end. The people of France were starving. There hud been bad harvests so that led tae food scarcity, an' of course they wanted a remedy an' the National Assembly's call tae revolt struck the masses as the perfect way tae resolve the problem. The people in oor country on the other hand," he firmly stated, "are no' starving. There is no reason fur them to revolt."

"That's true," his father reasoned.

"An' as far as I can see," John continued, "it would serve nae purpose fur us tae revolt in this country."

"Aye. Maybe. Bit if these societies fur reform are set up, I canna see how the government can ignore them. I mean – look at the recent riots in Dundee. Three days o' them, an' burning an effigy o' Dundas. He hud better watch oot. There's a mood afloat and he wid be wise tae take heed o' it."

"Why? He's the most powerful man in the country. The forces o' law an' order are in his hand. His nephew fur heaven's sake is the Lord Advocate. 'An' all he has tae dae is instruct the Magistrates tae arrest anybody who is causing disorder."

"That smacks of despotism," his father angrily retorted. "Nithin' more. Nithin' less."

"Pa," his mother interrupted, "let's change the subject. John hae jist arrived. Let's mak' his stay a restful one. Please let's no discuss politics whilst he's here."

"Very well Ma."

"Maybe John cuid help ye this week?"

"Aye. If you're up fur it John. I wid indeed be grateful fur your help."

"Whit's tae be done?"

"Guns hae tae be cleaned fur the shoot in a few weeks. I dinnae ken how many guests they're expecting but lest year there were nine, sae we hae tae assume there will be at least that number."

"Onythin' else?"

"We're huvin' a problem wi' foxes gaun after the pheasants. We'll hae tae set a few snares an' shoot a few crows."

"Nae problem" responded John. He would have liked to have followed in his father's footsteps and have worked his way up to 'under-keeper', but Lord Hugh employed sufficient people on the estate and the job would have only become available if his father died - and he certainly didn't wish for that. He enjoyed spending time with his father. He was a wise man and the conversation that week didn't revert back to politics so John was able to immerse himself in country life once more.

XI

On the morning of John Taylor's trial, William and Malcolm, along with the Advocates who were involved in the case, were pacing the vast Parliament Hall, with its magnificent oak panel-beamed roof. It was the Advocates tradition when discussing the merits of a case and the arguments they are going to present that they pace in contemplation wearing their traditional wigs and black gowns.

"The Lord Advocate has a persuasive case," said William as he got into step with Malcolm, "but it depends on the presiding judge. If it's Braxfield then he's sure to be found guilty."

"I hope the jurors have been fairly picked," Malcolm paused. "Braxfield has a penchant for choosing his own."

"We'll soon find out if it's him."

"And Adam Gillies is a good defence agent."

"Maybe," William reluctantly conceded, "but you have to consider the influence the Lord Advocate's uncle has in the courts. And if he's being charged as the ringleader of the riot he must have sufficient evidence."

"I hope so," replied his friend. "I hope it's not a trumped-up charge because they were keen to charge somebody."

"I doubt that," William commented as they continued pacing. "It would be difficult for the Crown to bring a case to the High Court of Justiciary if they didn't feel confident they had sufficient evidence to warrant a guilty verdict."

"We'll see," responded his friend.

They approached the far end of the Hall. Malcolm glanced up to the entrance of the courts and noticed Dundas and Gillies and their associates already walking in that direction. It was time for the trial to begin.

"We'd better go in," he said to his companion and they retraced their steps to follow their colleagues into the court room.

They saw as they entered that only a few were present. The Crown and Defence Advocates, the Clerk of the court, a court reporter and, they presumed, a reporter from the *Caledonian Mercury* sat on the right hand edge of the front row of the gallery. The gallery would usually have been packed with members of the public, but reception had been told to not admit any members of the public to this particular case and that to say it was a 'closed' court. Nevertheless, there was a clamour outside.

William and Malcolm sat in the gallery. Facing them, a side door opened at the top far left hand side and one of his Lordships entered.

"Court rise," the Clerk announced.

They all rose, while the judge settled himself on his bench, elevated at the top of the court room. It wasn't Lord Braxfield. The clerk then went over to another side door, and ushered the fifteen jurors into the court. When they had all entered, the judge asked them to remain standing and to raise their right hand. He then solemnly addressed the group. "Do you swear by Almighty God that you will well and truly try the accused and give a true verdict according to the evidence." The jurors replied as one, "We do." Each juror was then asked to repeat after the clerk "I … do solemnly, sincerely and truly declare and affirm that I will well and truly try the accused and give a true verdict according to the evidence." After they had been individually sworn in, they seated.

The accused, John Taylor, was led into the court from the cell below and directed to stand in the dock, facing the Judge.

The Judge addressed the gentlemen of the jury. "You are aware of the charges against the panel John Taylor." He then addressed the Lord Advocate and, in a solemn tone, said, "You may now proceed."

The Lord Advocate and his team had produced three witnesses. William and Malcolm listened intently to Adam Gillies' cross examination of the principal witness, the Captain of the 53rd regiment who was in command of soldiers at the riot.

"What approach did your regiment use to enter St Andrew Square?" asked Gillies.

"South St David's Street," the Captain replied.

"Then what did you command your regiment to do?"

"There was a riotous mob in the square. We could hear shouts of 'set fire to the sentry boxes.' I could see boxes positioned close to the Lord Provost's house. We had to act quickly to curb the riot. I immediately commanded my men to disperse the crowd and get to the house as quickly as possible."

"Did they obey your command?" Gillies asked.

"They did."

"And where were you at that moment?"

"At the back of the regiment."

"There was a crowd of about two thousand people. That is a lot of people in such a small place like St Andrew Square. They must have been crowded together," Gillies reasoned.

"They were," the Captain agreed.

"Your view then of those at the front of the house must have been distant. Would you describe your view of the front of the house as being distant Captain?"

"Perhaps."

"And when at the back of the mob, did you hear any voice above others?"

"Yes I did." And feeling more confident the Captain continued. "There was a man atop of another's man's shoulders, at the front beside the Lord Provost's house. He was gesticulating in the direction of the Lord Provost's house and we heard him commanding the crowd to set fire to the sentry boxes."

"From where you were at the back of the mob, did you get a clear view of the man atop another man's shoulders?"

"I did," the Captain firmly responded.

"Over the heads of up to two thousand people, you can say with certainty you had a clear view of the man's face?"

"I can," he confidently replied.

"You must have remarkable vision Captain to identify someone at that distance."

"I have good sight" the Captain retorted.

"Captain, in your opinion, how would you describe a working man's face?" Gillies asked.

The Captain contemplated for a moment then responded, "They mostly have beards"

"Gentlemen of the jury, as most of the working men have beards, could not any of them resemble the man in the dock? Is it not possible the witnesses were unsure as to who the leader was and decided John Taylor would do? He does admit to being present at the riot – for which he has much regret. And you said in your statement Captain that the man atop of a man's shoulders was wearing a rough, hairy or fur cap. But would not many men at St Andrew Square in the evening of the sixth June be wearing a rough, hairy or fur cap?"

Addressing the Captain again, he asked, "How then could you say – beyond reasonable doubt – that the man, whose back you saw, not his face, was indeed the man sitting in the dock?"

The Captain paused then said, "I can't."

"Why then did you put yourself forward as a witness if you could not be absolutely sure it was John Taylor on another man's shoulders shouting the command?"

The Captain, still maintaining his rigid stance, again hesitated.

"Take your time Captain," Gillies paused. "Remember you are under oath."

Eventually the Captain responded, "I saw a man two days later in the High Street whom I was convinced was the leader of the rioters. Not only was he wearing a rough cap, and had a beard, but it was the way he was gesticulating to the person he was speaking to – just like the man at the head of the riot."

Gillies, in a ponderous tone said, "I think it can be agreed in this court room that many working men in this city wear rough, hairy or fur caps and have beards. So, Captain," said Gillies, turning to smirk at the jurors, "can you now say with absolute certainty that John Taylor, the man in the dock, was the leader of the riot?"

"I am sure he was," the Captain responded with conviction.

"Thank you Captain. I have no further questions."

The Judge then addressed the jury. "Gentlemen you have heard the evidence presented. The court will now recess until ten o'clock tomorrow morning when you will have the opportunity of reviewing the evidence amongst yourselves, and consequently deliberating your verdict." He paused. "I wish you all to rise." They all rose. "Raise your right hand," the Judge pointedly told them, "and swear on the bible you will not discuss with anyone any of the proceedings you have heard in court today. If you do, you will be sent to prison." He adjusted the papers in front of him, picked up the bundle and rose. The Clerk of the Court immediately announced, "Court rise." After the Judge had left, the newspaper reporter hurriedly vacated the court room to get his copy in.

As they were walking towards the exit through Parliament Hall, Malcolm turned to Williams and said, "Gillies's defence was very good. He decimated the credibility of the Captain's evidence."

"We'll see," responded William "Robert is in a powerful position. I'd be surprised if the Judges weren't swayed by his evidence."

XII

Caledonian Mercury JULY 14th 1792 – High Court of Justiciary

Trial of John Taylor charged with being leader and instigator of the mob.

John Taylor, Panel.

'After the examination of witnesses in this trial, the Lord Advocate summed up the evidence on the part of the Crown, as did Mr Gillies for the panel. After which, the Jury were charged by the Lord Justice Clerk, and then they enclosed. Yesterday (13th July) they returned their verdict, finding, by a plurality of voices, the panel NOT GUILTY. He was of consequence dismissed from the bar.'

On the day the verdict was published John decided to take a stroll in the forest by himself. He wanted to commune with nature, immerse himself in the stillness of the forest, and transport himself back to those happy days of his childhood. He had of course mentioned nothing to his parents about his involvement with the riot. That was all past and he wanted to recover his spiritual energy to cope with the inevitable political turbulence there would be in the city when he returned.

He got to the edge of the forest and started to wander down the familiar path. New saplings had emerged since he had last visited and their virgin leaves looked tender in the dappled sunlight. With not a whisper of wind, the only sounds were his boots crackling dry twigs on the path. As he wandered further into the forest he noticed there was now an abundance of dog rose, enchanter's nightshade and honeysuckle. He stopped, breathed deeply and absorbed the atmosphere, disturbed only by a foraging solitary red-cockaded woodpecker – the soft drumming sound produced by vibrating its tongue on the tree surface. Perfectly contented, he continued on, passing many favourite trees he had climbed in his youth with Amelia. His father had pointed out how the forest abounded with natural produce – hazelnuts, hawthorn berries, comfrey, brides root, plantain and wood gavel. Those were happy days he recalled.

As he was reminiscing, he heard the sound of far-off laughter. He walked in the direction of where it was coming from and came upon a clearing which offered him an unobstructed view onto the vast lawn of the big house. Two young ladies were strolling on the lawn and although the laughter was distinctly Amelia's, he couldn't equate it with the beautiful image it was coming from. She had completely transformed into a stunning, elegant woman. The last time he had seen Amelia she had had her golden hair wrapped in plaits. But now, golden curled locks draped around her neck. He thought she looked a vision of beauty in her printed floral dress with a spencer jacket and her large pink rimmed straw bonnet, with ribbons on the top which bobbed as she spoke animatedly with her companion. He longed to rush up to her, find out what she had been doing in the intervening years, but he knew he couldn't. Their lives had taken them on their predictable separate courses and those halcyon summer days spent together had long since passed. All that remained were lingering memories of a joyful period in his youth.

He strode purposefully back through the forest to his home. He didn't mention anything to his parents. There was no point. Their childhood friendship could never be rekindled.

On the Saturday the verdict was published, William and Malcolm were at the Musselburgh races, being held on Leith Sands.

"Have you seen John Taylor's verdict?" Malcolm asked.

"Yes," said William. "I must say I was surprised he got off."

"Well. I wasn't," replied Malcolm and they huddled together so as not be overheard. "Gillies had presented a persuasive defence. The Captain was not credible. That's why they returned a not guilty verdict. The evidence was too circumstantial. There wasn't a positive identification. Many working men wear the same clothes he allegedly wore. But that's all they had to go on. They couldn't positively identify his facial features. Without that, you don't have a case." He paused. "I would have expected the Lord Advocate to have done his homework more thoroughly. I think he probably assumed, because of who he is, he would get away with presenting only circumstantial evidence. It was preposterous he thought he had a strong case."

"Yes. The Captain's evidence was slim."

"It was. You see Robert's problem is his arrogance."

"That's a very strong statement to make," Wiliam indignantly responded.

"But it's true. He presumed because of the influence of his uncle that the Judges and the jury would rule in his favour. Foolish man."

"Certainly, he won't be pleased with a not guilty verdict. Dundas is keen to show the public he will stamp out any insurgents and this verdict isn't going to help his cause. Still, we've got Bertram and Locke's trial next week."

"That's the accused for the riot in George Square. Who's for the Crown?"

"The Solicitor General. And Thomas Muir is defending Locke."

"Muir's good. He can usually present a persuasive case for a defendant."

"Yes," agreed William. "He can. But he's gathering a reputation for being an agent provocateur in this reform movement, and so the judges may well not favour what he has to say in Locke's defence." He lowered his head and huddled close to Malcolm. "Robert came to my lodgings last night. This is confidential – understood?"

"Of course."

"Rumour has it that Lord Daer, the Earl of Buchan and other nobles are to have a meeting at Fortune's Tavern on the twenty sixth of this month."

"What for?" asked Malcom.

"They're setting up a Friends of the People society, modelled on the lines of the Irish movement. Now, Robert's uncle wants agents to be present at the meeting to take a note of who is there. He doesn't want any momentum to be attached to this meeting."

"Fair enough."

"And," William continued, still speaking in a low voice, "he would like one of the agents to report directly to me."

"Why so?"

"He knows my views. I don't want the establishment to be rocked by discord, by rebellers. I'm quite clear about that."

"So you're going to become one of Dundas's lackey's," Malcolm retorted with a cynical air.

Affronted William said, "That's a bit harsh Malcolm."

"Well it's true. That's what you'll be."

"Maybe. But I want to progress in my career and if I become, as you say, a lackey, so be it. I see it as an auspicious way of advancing my career."

"My goodness," responded Malcolm, shocked by William's comment. "I didn't know you were that ruthless."

"I prefer the word ambitious. Anyway," said William, adopting a jovial stance, "let's drink a toast to progression."

XIII

The verdict in Taylor's trial was a relief to many including John and he anticipated the result of the Bertram and Locke trial on the nineteenth where they were both charged with throwing stones at the soldiers on the night of the riot at George Square. That evening he met his friend Peter in Fortune's tavern. It was his favourite in Stamp-office Close, down the High Street from his work. He opened the door and was immediately greeted with the pungent smell of unwashed bodies, a fug of tobacco smoke and stale ale. Pandemonium, it was packed with men from all walks of life – lawyers, labourers, judges, advocates, tradesmen. Some were playing cards and dice games.

Others were engaged in conversation or telling bawdy jokes which could be heard amidst much laughter. Others could be seen flirting in a drunken state with the women servers who took it all in good humour as they bustled about the busy tavern carrying drinks. Searching for Peter through the crowd John saw him seated at a long wooden table, tankards at the ready reading a paper.

"How's it gaun?" he asked his friend, as he sat down and joined him.

"Guid thanks," Peter replied putting the paper aside. "Hae ye heard the news?" Peter was a caddie in Edinburgh. Ostensibly messenger boys, they not only were familiar with every nook and cranny in the city, they knew where every resident lived and would know when a stranger arrived in the city. An organised society, caddies were subject to regulation and supervision by the Town Council and a prerequisite for the job was that they were literate, honest and reliable. They were also privy to the latest gossip and scandal.

"Ye mean Bertram and Locke?"

"Aye."

"I had tae typeset the result of the trial. I wis shocked wi the decision aboot Locke," John said to his friend.

"Aye. It wis a scandal. Tae be banished tae Botany Bay fur fourteen years fur allegedly throwing a stane at the sodjers in George Square."

Indignantly, John said, "Unbelievable. Nain o' the witnesses gave a positive identification o' his face, only his livery outfit. Bit Bertram wis also wearing a livery outfit. Yin o' the Crown witnesses wis in George Square on the evening o' the riot, an' he wis asked tae look at the prisoners, an' then asked if he recognised them. Well, he said he thought Bertram wis the person he saw throwing a stone, bit when he wis speaking tae the ither witnesses afore they went intae court an' conferring memories o' the event, he realised he wasnae sure if it wis him after all."

"So he wis turned by the other witnesses?"

"An' Bertram wis found not guilty." Getting animated John continued: "Bit Locke's employer, Mrs Ogg, gave a guid account saying he wis honest, reliable. An' no jist that, she said that on the day o' the riot he had been in the country wi a chaise an' came hame aboot six in the evening an' aboot seven he had heard aboot a riot in George Square an' went out tae see whit wis gaun on. Bit he came back aboot quarter of an hour later an' said to her daughter – who wis gaun tae gang oot – that she shouldn't gang fur there were ower mony folk oot an' that it cuid be dangerous fur her."

"So he wis looking oot fur the daughter?"

"Aye he wis. Then she sent Locke to the New Town tae fetch anither o' her daughters who wis visiting a friend there, an' when he wis coming back they passed by the Tron kirk. That wis it. Yin o' the soldiers recognised his livery outfit an' identified him as being the person who had thrown a stane at them. Bit her daughter corroborated her Mother's story an' said he wis only absent fir about a quarter o' an hour efter he told her not tae visit the Square. An' …she also said that when he returned she saw him git corn frae her faither tae feed the horses." He furrowed his brow and said, "Bit despite the fact nain o' the witnesses recognised his face, the Solicitor General dismissed Muir's defence pleadings an' told the court that as three witnesses gave positive proof against Locke, an' twa ithers corroborated their evidence, that constituted direct an' positive proof o' the guilt against Locke. An' the jury unanimously found him guilty. Och, it's awfy upsetting when innocent people receive such a sentence fur a crime they obviously didnae commit."

"Aye. Bit Dundas is doing everything he possibly can tae send a message tae us all - that he's no gaun tae tolerate ony unruly behaviour. An' if that means sending an innocent man tae exile ....whit can we dae?"

Huddled together and absorbed in their conversation they hadn't taken heed of the stranger sitting opposite until he leant forward and said to them in a low voice,

"Ye can join the movement. That's whit ye can dae."

"Whit?" John retorted.

"I repeat," the stranger said, "ye can join the reform movement."

John put his arms on the table and, whispering, leant towards the man. "I dinnae think ye should be talking aboot that here."

"Why no?" the man replied. "It's on everybody's lips. It's the only way tae stop Dundas an' his tyrannous ways."

John and Peter looked at one another, unsure as to whether to engage the man in conversation.

"I overheard whit ye were saying aboot Locke," the stranger continued. "It's a scandal. An' Muir did a grand job defending him – he disnae charge folk that cannae afford it ye ken. He's a guid man. Bit the Lordships will continue tae over-rule his pleadings because they've been told he's on the side o' reform, an' wi' their interests an' friendships wi the landed gentry, they're no gaun tae cow-tow tae ony o' his arguments."

"How dae ye ken this?" John asked.

"I hae friends in various places. They keep me informed." He took a long, hard look at John and eventually said, "Dae I nae ken ye?"

Startled. John hastily responded, "I dinnae think so."

The man looked into the distance, was silent for a moment and then became animated. "Aye. I remember," he enthusiastically said. "I handed ye a pamphlet at St Andrew Square."

"I wasnae there," John immediately responded.

Emphatic the stranger said, "Aye ye wur. I recognise ye noo. I ne're forget a face."

Aghast Peter looked at John, "Ye wurnae there ..... wur ye?"

"Aye he wis," the man responded. "As I say, I ne'er forget a face."

John, lowering his head towards the man said, "Cuid ye keep yer voice doon."

The man did as he was asked. "Nothing tae be ashamed aboot."

"It wis an accident," John told him. "I dinnae want tae think aboot it. C'mon Peter, let's finish up an' gang awa."

Peter and John hastily finished their drink and as they stood up to leave the man said, "My name is Donald. I'll see ye again lads. There's a meeting on the ninth of August at the White Hart Inn in the Grassmarket. Ye shuid come alang."

"I dinnae think so," responded John and he hastily left.

When they got outside Peter glanced from left to right to see if there was anybody about. Nobody. He turned to John and said, "Whit in God's name were ye daein' at the riot?"

"It wis an accident."

"Well, ye wur lucky ye wurnae arrested. Yer a fool."

"It jist seemed a lark. I dinnae want tae talk aboot it."

"An' rightly so," his friend gravely responded.

They bade farewell and went their separate ways. Peter to the right, up to the top of the High Street to tout for caddie business, John in the opposite direction to his lodgings. As he walked back his mind was fraught with anxiety. Why on earth didn't he lie to the man? Why didn't he say it was mistaken identity – it definitely wasn't him? It would have been so easy to have said that, except he knew he was innately honest. He couldn't help blurting out it was an accident. If only he had had the presence of mind to take a deep breath when the man said I never forget a face – pause – reflect for a moment before responding. But Peter was his friend, and he couldn't lie to him. Although now how he wished he had. The truth can't be reversed. And what a blow to be recognised. It never occurred to him that would happen so many weeks after the event. He couldn't change his appearance, but he would never discuss it again with Peter, he was resigned about that. The only positive action he could take was to not return to Fortune's for a while and be nowhere near the Grassmarket on the seventh of August. He would never meet that stranger again and wanted nothing to do with the reform movement. He had a good job. He was settled with his lodgings. He didn't want to get involved with anything that would jeopardise his life. He would make an effort to put the whole thing behind him and go about his business as if nothing had happened. That decided, he started to breathe less rapidly and carried on walking down the hill at a more relaxed pace, convincing himself that all would be well.

XIV

On the evening of the twenty-sixth of July, William was pacing the floor of the front room in his lodgings waiting for Jock to return from the meeting at Fortune's. What William found disturbing was the fact so many members of the nobility were on this fight for burgh reform. He couldn't fathom why they would want their heritage, with all the advantageous accoutrements - political and social - disrupted. What were the benefits of altering the status quo? He couldn't see the advantages at all. What could peasants contribute to the social and intellectual life of society? His musings were interrupted when he heard footsteps on the landing. He retrieved his pocket watch and glanced at the time. Ten thirty. It must be Jock. He heard a knock at the door, marched over to it and briskly opened it. A stranger stood before him. "You're Jock, I presume?"

"Aye. I am," responded the man.

When Jock entered William rapidly shut the door behind him and ushered him into the front room. "You have the list?" he pointedly asked.

Jock, standing next to him passed over a piece of paper and said, "Aye. It wis weel attended. There were mony nobles there as ye'll see frae the list. There's mony a name a wisnae able to tak doon bit Ah'll be able tae recognise most people agin."

Quickly scrolling down the list William wasn't surprised to see the names of Henry Erskine, his brother the Earl of Buchan and the advocate George Wallace. Looking at Jock he asked, "What was said at the meeting?"

Without hesitation Jock responded. "That we shuid a' fight fur th' richt tae hae voting reform. An'," he retrieved another piece of folded paper from his jacket pocket, "we were gien this at the door whin we arrived. It's Lord Daer's proposed letter tae Charles Grey tae repeal the Act o' Union fur the benefit o' oor land ..."

"What" exclaimed William and snatched the paper out of Jock's hand '*Lord Daer's letter to Charles Grey MP.*' He quickly glanced at the first few words 'Scotland has long groaned under the chains of England ...' He stopped reading and dismissively commented, "What a preposterous idea. For your interest Jock, it was Charles Grey, along with his Whig aristocratic cohorts, who in early April of this year, founded the first Friends of the People Society. He rather ridiculously argued that the reform of the parliamentary system would remove public complaints and restore the tranquillity of the nation, and stressed that the Friends of the People would not become involved in any activities that would promote public disturbance. And then at the end of that month, he introduced a parliamentary reform bill. Pitt, quite rightly, argued that any reform at this time would give encouragement to the Radicals who were supporting the French Revolution. And how right he was. Just look at the recent riots. Anyway Jock, more importantly, was a date made for another meeting?"

"Not specifically, bit they said it wid probably be in a few weeks' time."

"Well, keep me informed. And if you have any news, when the courts resume in early September you could leave a note in my pigeonhole at Parliament Square. Come through the main entrance, at the end of the Hall you'll see double doors, go through them and the pigeonholes are directly in front of you. And if there is anything urgent, you could drop a note through my letter-box."

"Aye sir. I wull."

William reached into his pocket, took out a coin and handed it to Jock.

"Thank ye sir."

Without another word, William showed him to the door. As soon as Jock had left he took the copy letter to his desk, lit a candle and sat down to peruse the contents. The letter began:

'Scotland has long groaned under the chains of England and knows that its connections there has been the cause of its greatest misfortunes. Perhaps you may shrug your shoulders at this and call it Scot's prejudice, but it is time at moments like these when much may depend on suiting measures to the humour of the people, that you Englishmen should see this rather as it is or at least be aware of how we Scotsmen see it.

We have existed a conquered province these two centuries. We trace our bondage from the Union of the Crowns and find it little alleviated by the Union of Kingdoms. What is it, you say, we have gained by the Union? Commerce, Manufacturers, Agriculture? Without going deep into the principles of political economy or asking how our Government or any country can give these to any nation, it is evident in this case that the last Union (1707) gave us little assistance in these, except removing a part of the obstacles which your greater power had posterior to the first Union (1603) thrown around us. But if it did more, what would that amount to, but to the common saying that we bartered our liberty, and with it our morals, for a little wealth.

You may say we have joined emancipation from feudal tyranny. I would believe most deliberately that had no Union ever taken place we should, in that respect, have been more emancipated than we are. Left to ourselves we should probably have had a progression towards liberty and not less than yours.

Our grievances prior to the accession of the Stewarts to your throne were of a kind which even had that event not taken place, must before this time have been annihilated. Any share of human evil that might have awaited us, we are ignorant of, where as we feel that we have under gone. Even to the last of our separate parliaments, they were always making laws for us and now and then one to remedy a grievance. And a people acquiring knowledge must have compelled a separate legislature to more of these.

Since the parliaments were united, scarcely four acts have been passed in as many score of years affecting Scots law or merely the incongruities which must arise betwixt old laws and modern manners.

As our courts of law find something of this to be necessary they, instead of applying to the parliament at London, have taken upon themselves, with a degree of audacity, which can hardly be made credible to a stranger, to make under pretence of regularity of court, little laws (acts of parliament as they call them) materially affecting the liberty of the subject.

Kept out of view by your greater mass so as never to make our conscience be the principle objects even to our own representatives at a distance, so as not to make our cries heard in the capital which alone awes an arbitrary government; our laws and customs different so as to make our grievances unintelligible; our law established distant so as to deprive us of the benefit of those constant circuits from the capital which, by rendering the learned and spirited defender of the laws, dwelling at the actual source of actual power, acquainted with the lesser transactions of the remotest corner of the country; provides, perhaps, the greatest remedy to a half free state against some of the bad consequences of extended territory.

Our civil establishment distinct, so as to isolate the petty tyranny of office; even our greed and national unity working to retain still more to leave you (our then only protectors, although oppressors) ignorant of internal situation. We have suffered the misery which is perhaps inevitable to a lesser and remote country in a junction where the Governing powers are united but the Nations are not united.

In short, thinking we have been the worse of every connection hitherto with you, the Friends of Liberty in Scotland have almost universally been enemies of the Union with England. Such is the fact, whether the reasons be good or bad.'

After reading it, William threw the letter onto the desk in disgust and started to ponder. If Daer was determined to use his influence that could pose problems. But what audacity that Lord Daer had. I'd rather bow to Parliament, William thought, than to people like him who want to completely disrupt the status quo and make aspersions about the creation of our laws which are to the benefit of him, and his like. And what a preposterous suggestion we repeal the Act of Union and sever contact from England. 'Petty tyranny of office' what a cheek. And implying the nations are not united? Of course they are. Is the man deranged? And who are these Friends of Liberty of Scotland? They are but a handful of noble renegades. That is all. But we shall need to influence newspapers in not publishing their demands. With that in mind, he walked through to his bed closet where he kept his clothes, and, as he was unfastening his cravat, remembered a lighter pursuit. Amelia. The courts recessed for the month of August and he had been invited to the partridge shoot on her father's estate. He wouldn't have normally been able to accept but, fortuitously, the first of September that year fell on a Saturday, so he was able to attend. Now that was something to look forward to.

XV

Dusk had already descended when William had arrived the night before. When he alighted the coach at the entrance of the driveway, he had no need of a lantern to guide his way up the poplar lined path as the beam of a full moon in the cloudless sky filtered through the branches of the trees and lit his way. He marvelled at the silence which was interrupted only by the occasional hoot of an owl and the crackling of dry twigs underfoot. As he approached the main entrance, he looked at the lawn the expanse of which was displayed by the light of the moon and espied a fox slinking across it. William thought if he had had a gun to hand, he would have shot it, but he would have enough practice in the morning. When he reached the door, he pulled the bell which was soon opened by Benjamin, carrying a candle.

"Good evening sir," he greeted William. "You had a good journey I hope?" he asked as he ushered him into the grand hall.

"Yes indeed. Thank you Benjamin." As he started to follow him, the grandfather clock in the hall began to strike the hour. It was ten o'clock.

"Lord Hugh is expecting you in the library. Would you like to put your bag in your room before you see his Lordship?" he asked as they mounted the stairs.

"Yes, that would be good. Thank you."

As they were proceeding up the stairs William remarked how quiet the house seemed.

"Well sir, Malcolm is working in his study, and Miss Amelia and Miss Charlotte have retired for the evening."

Stifling his disappointment that Amelia had already retired, he managed to calmly respond, "I don't think I've met Miss Charlotte."

"You will at dinner tomorrow, sir."

On hearing that, William immediately perked up at the thought of seeing Amelia and jovially responded, "I look forward to that."

As they were approaching the bed chamber Benjamin turned and said, "We didn't think it necessary to put a fire on in your room sir. We seem to have what I believe is called an Indian summer."

"Yes. It is remarkably warm for this time of year."

When they entered the candlelit bed chamber William plopped his hat on the bed, laid his bag on the chest at the foot of it, unfastened the clasps and started to unpack. The first thing he took out were his low-heeled pointed shoes which had been placed on a newspaper at the top of the bag to stop them getting squashed. The detachable clasp was inside one of the shoes, and he laid them on the floor. Next, he retrieved from a compartment his newly tailored beige knitted silk breeches. William was glad the fashion favoured tight breeches because he had athletic legs and was delighted to display them to the best advantage. And he wanted to impress Amelia and turn her head in his direction. He laid them on the chest then took out a white linen shirt. Benjamin, who was drawing the drapes, glanced over to him, and noticing the shirt looked somewhat crumpled enquired, "Shall I ask Alice to press that sir?"

"Yes," replied William, still unpacking, "I would be grateful if you did. And some other things please. The breeches are slightly creased and shirt and trousers for church on Sunday could also do with a press."

"Lay them on the chair sir, and Alice will pick them up in the morning." Benjamin said as he walked to the door. "Are you ready to see his Lordship sir?"

"Should I change?" asked William, still wearing his dark every day coat skirt.

Benjamin looked at him benignly. "No. His Lordship won't mind if you don't. It's late. We will all be retiring soon. We have an early start in the morning."

"Yes," replied William enthusiastically. "I'm looking forward to the shoot," and he followed Benjamin along the corridor to the library.

"Come in!" shouted Lord Hugh when he heard a knock at the door. "William. Thank you, Benjamin." And turning to William he said, "Delighted to see you. Would you like a glass of port or claret?"

"Claret thank you sir," William replied as his host laid his book down, rose from his chair at the back of the desk and came to greet him.

They shook hands heartily and Lord Hugh signalled for him to sit in one of the easy chairs in front of the desk. "Did you have a good journey?" he asked as he walked to the chest to pour William a glass.

"It was excellent thank you sir."

Lord Hugh smiled. "Mrs MacPherson thought you would be a little hungry after your journey so she prepared something for you." And there it was on a supper table, adjacent to William's chair. He settled into the chair, as Lord Hugh laid a glass on the table and sat in an identical one opposite, and picked up a plate.

"You have an opportunity to sample Mrs MacPherson's oatcakes," Lord Hugh proudly pronounced. "And her delicious apple chutney. And some local cheese. That should suffice I think."

"Yes. It certainly will sir," responded William picking up an oatcake, knife and butter. William had met Lord Hugh on many occasions and felt comfortable in his presence and like John, he was deeply impressed by the volume of books stacked on the shelves. Curious to know what book Lord Hugh had been reading when he arrived, he asked him.

"Nothing to do with business," his Lordship nonchalantly replied. "Bit of leisure time this evening. I'm re-reading Candide."

"Oh," remarked William, slightly surprised at the choice.

Looking pensive Lord Hugh responded, "We are living in troubled times William." He paused. "I admire Voltaire's philosophy. 'One should see the world clearly, and do whatever good one can.' That is an important stance to take in life. Don't you think William?"

"Yes of course sir. We should all adhere to that philosophy," William quickly responded.

"Glad you agree William," his host replied, casually crossing his legs and relaxing into his chair. "Now. How have you been spending your time this past month?"

William, hurriedly trying to swallow his food said, "I've been staying at a friend's estate most of the time."

"And where is it?" his host pleasantly enquired.

"Near Dumfries."

"I might well know the man. What's his name?"

"Neil Grant. But I don't think you will know him sir. He's a fellow advocate. He has a manager to run his estate as he is not often there."

"Um. I don't know the name. And what did you do there?"

William smiled. "Practice my shooting sir."

"Crows. I presume?"

"Yes. His estate is particularly suitable for pheasants and we wanted to reduce the crow numbers to preserve as many eggs as we could."

"Good idea," retorted his host. "But partridges are somewhat smaller than crows William, so… good luck tomorrow," he smiled.

"Well, I'll give it my best shot," William replied, moderately irked by the comment.

"It's a good way to conclude your break. Are you looking forward to getting back into court?"

"Yes. I suppose I am. But, as always, it's good to re-energise the system and start afresh."

"It is always important to be able to disconnect from the stresses and strains of life," Lord Hugh responded.

"Indeed it is."

"And I suppose you and Malcolm will resume your social life when you return to the city."

"Yes. I expect we will."

"But are you not thinking about marrying William? You're of an age."

"Actually sir, it is something I am starting to perhaps think about."

"Who's the lucky woman to have such a dashing young man as you?"

"That's flattering sir. Thank you." He looked slightly uncomfortable when he added, "I'd rather not say."

"Up to you William. But as we think of you as part of the family, I'm sure we will soon hear about it."

"Indeed. And how has Malcolm been? I believe he's doing some work," William remarked, almost finishing his supper.

"Yes. We too have had a busy time on the estate, but he was keen to do some preparation for a case to be heard next week and looks forward to seeing you in the morning."

"That's why I arrived late. I too had to do some preparation for next week. But tomorrow will be just good sport."

"And it looks like we will have a good day. Certainly it was a clear sky, and no wind when I last looked out."

"It's a beautiful evening. Very still. And mild. Yes. Tomorrow should be fine."

"Yes of course," and noticing that William was eating the last oatcake kindly asked, "Are you soon ready for bed? Or would you like another glass?"

"No thank you sir. I won't have another drink. I am tired. It's been a long day," and he rested his plate on the supper table and stood up. Lord Hugh followed.

"Delighted you could make it William," Lord Hugh told him as they were walking towards the door. "I shall see you in the morning. Seven fifteen. Sharp. Benjamin has told Alice to wake you at six thirty."

"Thank you sir. And I am delighted to be here." When the door was opened into the corridor they wished one another a good night as they went in opposite directions to their rooms.

The following morning Alice tapped gently at the door at six thirty and whispered, "Can a come in sir?"

"Yes," William drowsily responded. She entered quietly carrying a candle, put it on the marble topped table by the fireplace and softly stepped to the window to open his drapes.

As the morning light filtered into the room he glanced at her and thought what a pretty little woman she was in her woven striped cotton gown. The inverted pleats at the back and the crisp white apron tied tightly round her form emphasised her slender waist. Her abundant head of hair was tucked neatly under her ruffled white cotton cap, trimmed with silk ribbon. A pleasant introduction to the day he thought as he looked out and beheld the sun rising over a groove in the Pentland hills.

"It's a rare mornin' sir," she timidly announced once they were opened. "Ah'll jist fetch yer water," and she went to retrieve the large, heavy ewer of warm water she had left outside which she placed beside the basin on the marble table when she returned. "Shall a pour the water into the basin noo sir?" she asked.

"No thank you. I'll do that shortly."

And, seeing the clothes draped on the arm of the chair, she picked them up and demurely asked "Is there onything else sir?"

"I did notice one of the brass buttons on my coat skirt was slightly loose ...."

"Would ye like me tae mend it sir?"

"Yes. If you would please. It's hanging on the hook by the door," William told her.

"Yes sir," she said, and picked up the coat and departed.

When the door was closed he raised himself from the bed and walked over to the commode to perform his daily functions. He then sauntered over to the wash basin, poured the water from the jug into it, threw off his night shirt and welcomed the warm water over his body. He vigorously dried himself, put on his undergarments, plus fours, a white shirt – whose creases were barely noticeable – a cravat, socks, then calf length leather boots. The maid then knocked on the door to return his coat. He looked at it and was impressed by her sewing. She had checked, and expertly secured all the buttons. He put it on, wound his hair back, so no loose hairs would tickle his face and distract his shot and, with his morning preparations thus completed, he left the room.

He approached the dining room as Lord Hugh and Malcom were coming along the corridor. "Good morning William," his host heartedly called out. "Sleep well?"

"Yes sir. Very well thank you. And Malcolm. Good to see you."

"And you. Looking forward to the shoot?" Malcolm asked as he opened the dining door for his father to enter.

"Indeed I am. It looks like we have perfect day for it."

"Yes" agreed Lord Hugh as he entered the dining room. "Beautiful sunrise. A good start. Now. Let's get our breakfast." And he went to the large, polished mahogany sideboard where a buffet awaited them, alongside a pleasing aroma of coffee which permeated the room.

A pot of porridge sat on a plate-warmer and there were kippers, lightly spiced buns flavoured with caraway seeds, buttered muffins and a variety of Mrs MacPherson's home-made jams. As Lord Hugh was serving himself and talking to Malcolm, William quickly glanced round the room. The décor was not dissimilar to the town house: the wood panels were painted dove grey and a variety of gold framed portraits and paintings adorned the walls, the largest of which was above the mantelpiece. It was of a beautiful, young woman whose expression was the essence of serenity. He presumed it to be Lord Hugh's wife. Continuing his brief browse, he admired the vast Turkish rugs with their unique patterns relating the individual weaver's story. And on either side of the room were placed console tables, each with a vase placed on top with an array of hydrangeas. The dining table he recognised as the most popular among the elite. Solid mahogany, it could with its extensions, accommodate up to fourteen people and William had a flicker of an image of himself entertaining in the room.

"I hear you've been practising your shot William?" Malcolm commented as he took his plate to the table.

"Yes. It's been a good break," he replied, helping himself to a bowl of porridge. "You know Neil Grant I presume?"

"Yes of course I do. Good man," Malcolm said, adding, "he's effective in court."

"Yes," agreed William. "He's very good."

They were all seated at the table and Lord Hugh said, "We must be in the courtyard at eight fifteen sharp. Mr Macleod and his sons, Charles and Edward will be joining us."

William smiled. "Was he a supporter of the Jacobean cause, I wonder?"

"That was years ago," Lord Hugh dismissively responded. "We never talk politics." He then smiled and said, "That's why we have remained good friends."

"Wise policy father," agreed his son. "Although it is difficult these days not to talk about politics. It's the main topic in chambers because of all the cases coming up. The first case I have to deal with when I go back is of an alleged revolutionary."

"That's a very strong word to use Malcolm," Lord Hugh chided his son. "I do not approve of it." Indignant, he continued, "There are no such thing as revolutionaries in our country. And if you're talking about men who seek reform, they are most assuredly not of revolutionary minds."

"Well," his son responded, "that is not what we are hearing at court. But …let's not talk about work. It's going to be a glorious day and we shall have a marvellous shoot."

"Yes," his father agreed. "That's the attitude to adopt. Now William, I presume you didn't bring a gun?"

"Quite right sir, I didn't." He smiled, "I thought it wouldn't be welcomed on the coach ride by the other passengers." They all smiled.

"Of course we've got a gun for you and a cartridge bag," said Lord Hugh. "Is there anything else you need?"

"I'm absolutely fine sir, thank you."

"Actually, thinking about coaches," Malcolm addressed William. "As there won't be one tomorrow, I presumed you thought we could ride back to Edinburgh after church."

"Apologies Malcolm. I should have dropped you a note. Yes, I did presume that."

"Fine. If we have good weather, like today, it should be a good ride."

"Let's get back to today, "said Lord Hugh, checking his watch. "Five minutes before we leave. Would you like another coffee William?"

"No thank you sir. I won't."

"And Malcolm?"

"No thank you father."

"Well then, let's get down to the courtyard."

XVI

On the morning of the shoot, Amelia was lying in bed thinking about how much she enjoyed being back at the estate away from city life. When she had arrived she had decided to take an interest in the news and avidly read the papers being delivered – The *Caledonian Mercury*, The Times and the Edinburgh Herald. The reform movement was, she saw, gathering momentum. Trees of Liberty were being set up in many of the cities and effigies of Dundas were being burned. But on a lighter note, her friend Charlotte, from the art class, had come to stay. After breakfast, they would set up easels in the morning room beside the window which overlooked the rose garden Bob had established many years before. The roses were in full bloom and created a stimulating visual image for the girls to be inspired by. The pride of the garden was the weeping rose tree, abundant with flowers that cascaded down. On a sunny morning, when the bright light streamed in,

Amelia would open the windows and anticipate inhaling the beautiful fragrances from the roses.

After lunch they would go for a ride. Jo, the groom, exercised the horses when they were in the city. Christie, a fifteen-hand hunter, was her favourite horse and when he galloped through the forest trails, she regained her carefree spirit and could temporarily abandon her learned poise. And some traditions had endured. Often after the ride, she and Charlotte would go to the kitchen garden and pick the ripe fruit, just as she and John had done, then go to the kitchen where a tray of Mrs MacPherson's freshly baked scones lay invitingly on the table, topped as they usually were with her mouth-watering jams, blackcurrant, gooseberry and raspberry.

Her solitude was interrupted when Meg came in to open her drapes. Amelia looked out and beheld a clear blue sky. She glanced across to the branches of a tall tree. They were still. There wasn't a whisper of breath in the wind. A perfect day for the shoot.

The party meanwhile, were congregating in the courtyard. "Ah. Mr Macleod," Lord Hugh called out enthusiastically when he saw him approaching. "Good to see you."

"Good to see you too sir," and held out his hand in greeting. "And we've got a good day for the shoot."

"Indeed we have," responded Lord Hugh. "You know Malcolm of course. And this is his friend William."

"How do you do," William said shaking hands.

"And these are my sons," Mr Macleod said in a proud tone. "Charles, the elder, and Edward. Actually," he looked at his youngest, "this is Edward's first time, so we'll see how it goes."

Edward looked abashed when his father made the comment and replied, "I'll do my best father. I've been doing a lot of practising, shooting crows with our game-keeper."

"Yes. He told me you were coming along. I'm sure you will do your best," his father encouragingly responded.

"Well, as I was saying to William last night," said Lord Hugh, "partridges are not such an easy target as crows. What to do is to pick up your gun as soon as the dogs are commanded to flush out coveys, get into a comfortable position for shooting when the dogs are searching, and as soon as a partridge flies over the stubble, take aim and quickly pull the trigger. It's a matter of concentration."

"Thank you for the advice sir," replied Edward.

"And thinking of the shoot," Lord Hugh turned towards a group of men in the corner of the courtyard where three springer spaniels were sitting alertly beside a pleasant looking, robust man. "Come William, let me introduce you to Robbie McCulloch, our gamekeeper." And they started to stroll in their direction. "We are very fortunate to have him. It takes at least two years to train a dog. And what patience you have to have, and perse-verance. He really is quite expert at it. Wait to see them in action. Superb quartering. He's even adopted his own whistling commands, and my goodness, they work. Ah. Morning Robbie."

"Morning sir," Robbie replied, smiling at him. "An' this is Peter and James who are helping this morning."

"Very good," said Lord Hugh, with a slight bow of his head.

William, standing straight with his hands clasped behind his back, looked at the spaniels and then to Robbie and said, "I hear they're good at quartering."

"They are indeed sir," agreed Robbie. He adopted a proud stance and said, "I coudnae ask fur better dogs," as he looked at his animals. "This yin is her first shoot," he pointed to a predominantly brown patched spaniel who looked up at him adoringly. "She's taken tae the concept o' flush an' retrieve like a duck takes tae water. So, we'll see how Heather goes the day."

"Indeed we will Robbie. Now, thinking of birds," said Lord Hugh emphatically, "let's get this shoot on its way. Peter, would you get the guns please, and the cartridge bags, and tell Joe and Mr McLeod's driver to bring the ponies and traps round."

"Right you are sir."

"And William, can you go inside and ask Benjamin to bring out the drinks?" Lord Hugh asked.

"Certainly sir." And as William started to briskly walk towards the front of the house, Benjamin emerged with a tray full of drinks.

"Perfect timing Benjamin," Lord Hugh shouted over to him as they walked back to the guest group. As they were downing their sloe gins, the traps arrived. "Right chaps. Let's go," announced Lord Hugh, and Peter handed out the guns and cartridges.

"I'll lead tae the first stubble field," said Robbie as he ushered his dogs onto to a trap, followed by Peter and James.

En route to their destination, Mr Macleod had a quiet word with Edward about the shoot. "It's the start of the season and this is a good introduction for you because the birds won't be accustomed to being disturbed, so they'll be slightly sluggish. And watch the dogs. They'll tell you when there are birds about. Their noses will go down and they'll go into overdrive when they scent a covey. And be prepared to shoot the moment the birds flush. Even when they lift at ten yards they can accelerate very fast. But the advantage of partridge shooting is when the covey is disturbed by the dogs they don't separate as quickly as pheasants do. And that gives you a better chance of a good shot. Understood?"

"Yes father," Edward quietly replied.

They arrived at the field, and when they had all disembarked, they followed Robbie who stopped in front of a low hedge, at the edge of the stubble. He turned and spoke to the party. "Afore we a' stand in a line, I jist want tae remind ye that when the birds are doon, hud the line stationary while the dogs are sent tae retrieve them, even if ye think there may be birds waiting tae flush ahead o' you. We've got a perfect day fur the shoot. There's no wind, so the birds wilnae be curling back. Noo – if ye wid a' space oot, aboot thirty yards apart - I'll sound the horn fur us tae begin."

"Just before we start," Lord Hugh interjected calling out, "Jo, could you bring our picnic lunch round about twelve thirty? If we're not here, we'll be in a nearby field." He then turned to the party and said, "Mrs MacPherson has made her delicious venison pie and raspberry tart. Now. Back to the shoot. There's no brace target. We'll just see how it goes. Enjoy." They separated from one another along the hedge and, once in position, awaited the blast of the horn. As soon as the dogs heard the sound of the horn, they ran off into to the stubble at a terrific speed and started to excitedly quarter to and fro in search of their quarry.

"There's one!" shouted Malcolm, and other birds started to take flight. And so the sport began.

* * * *

Amelia and Charlotte were getting dressed for dinner in Amelia's bedchamber which overlooked the courtyard when they heard the clatter of hooves approaching. "The party is returning," Amelia called out gleefully. "I wonder how they got on?" And she hurriedly went to the window and peeked out. "Father looks pleased with himself," she smiled, and turning to Charlotte, said, "Come and see." Charlotte did as she was bid and excitedly looked out at the group as they were getting out of their traps. But it wasn't Lord Hugh she looked at, it was the man standing next to him who caught her eye. "Is that William beside your father?" "Yes," replied her friend.

"Gosh," Charlotte exclaimed, "isn't he handsome?"

Amelia contemplated for a moment then said, "Yes. I suppose he is." She paused. "But I'm not sure about his attitude. He was a bit abrasive the last time we met."

Then they heard Lord Hugh call out, "Well done with the dogs Robbie."

"Yes," agreed William, "well done. They did themselves proud today, particularly Heather. I look forward to next year's shoot."

The group then started to disperse, each person going into the house to change for dinner. "Well," said Amelia to Charlotte, "we'll soon find out how his attitude is this evening. Come, let's get ready."

When the dinner gong was rung at five, Amelia and Charlotte hurriedly left their room and proceeded down the stairs. William was standing in the hall and cheerfully greeted her as she descended. "Hello Amelia. I heard you had company."

"Yes William," she nonchalantly responded as they reached the foot of the stairs. "This is my friend Charlotte. I don't think you've met."

William nodded his head and courteously acknowledged her friend. "How do you do," he said. "And how have you ladies been spending your day?"

"Charlotte and I have had a lovely day painting," she told him. "It was a glorious, balmy day so we set up our easels outside and had a marvellous time. But how was the shoot?" she asked as they walked towards the dining room. "We glanced out of the window when everyone arrived back, and you all looked pleased with yourselves."

"Yes. It was good fun," said William enthusiastically as they strolled into the dining room. Benjamin and his assistant were at the sideboard where an array of food was displayed on plate warmers, awaiting to be served: fish, venison, roast beef. At the centre was placed an elegant soup tureen, and jellies and a selection of cheeses were placed at the side. Lord Hugh, who was standing with the others by the fireplace, having overheard the comment gleefully responded. "Yes. It was indeed. We had a great day, and the weather was perfect. We didn't have a target. But it was a great success, we got in a total of thirteen brace."

Surprised, Amelia said, "That's a lot."

"Yes it is. But of course it was the start of the season, which makes them a little easier to shoot. Now," he said, addressing his daughter, "let me introduce you to Mr Macleod's sons, Charles and Edward. And this is Amelia's friend, Miss Charlotte." Once they had graciously acknowledged one another, Lord Hugh stepped towards the table and, as he was sitting down, said:

"Amelia you sit by my side and William opposite. And the others, please seat yourselves."

Benjamin brought the tureen to the table and the assistant started to serve. The men were hungry so they all ate in silence for several minutes until Lord Hugh asked Amelia, "Did you have a good day my dear?"

"We did father thank you. We were painting in the garden all day. It was perfect."

Charlotte, who was sitting next to Amelia agreed. "We couldn't have asked for a better day. It was indeed perfect."

"And so was ours," Lord Hugh enthusiastically responded and resumed his report of the day. "Well done to you all. I was pleasantly surprised as to how good you were. And well done Edward, shooting your first bird. Did you enjoy it?"

"Yes, I did sir."

"And I think you shot more than one?"

"Yes," Edward replied, looking pleased with himself. "I shot three sir."

"Well done. It's difficult to maintain concentration for that length of time. Did you find it waning at the end?"

"Yes I did sir. A little."

"Well, no doubt you will be practising with a few pheasant shoots. You'll become a dab hand with a gun soon enough. And you're welcome to join us next year," hastily adding, "and of course you as well Charles."

"Thank you sir," replied Charles.

The soup bowls were removed and replaced with plates and whilst the assistant butler served the trout, Benjamin went round the table pouring white wine into glasses, apart from Edward, who declined.

"The trout. Is it from the estate?" Mr Macleod pleasantly asked his Lordship. "Yes," replied Lord Hugh. "Robbie has got two men from the estate working the river. They're very good. Although occasionally I'm sure they take one or two. But I don't mind. It's only to be expected."

"Do you have a problem with poachers?" asked William.

"Robbie is very good at keeping an eye on everything," his host responded.

"And delightful wine," Mr Macleod declared after his first sip. "What is it Lord Hugh?"

"Pinot Gris. It is perfect with fish," he declared and started to eat. After a few minutes he said, "It is not being produced like it used to be you know. The traditional owners of vineyards in France started to be removed when the turmoil began with the new regime, but fortunately we had a substantial stock of it so – enjoy."

Not wanting to engage in political discussion, Malcolm changed the conversational tack and commented, "Weren't the dogs effective today?"

"They were indeed," Mr Macleod enthusiastically agreed. "My goodness, what a good gamekeeper you have Lord Hugh. The dogs were so adept at quartering. I've never seen such impressive work."

"Yes," piped up Edward. "They were thrilling to watch. I'd never seen game dogs in action before. I really was impressed."

"I was telling William this morning how good Robbie is at training them. We couldn't do without him."

Benjamin came to remove the plates, replace them with others and then produced the venison. His assistant served whilst Benjamin poured the red wine.

"My goodness, Lord Hugh. You do have a good wine cellar. Now what is this red wine?" asked Mr Macleod.

"Ah. One of my favourites. Again, it's French. It's a burgundy claret. Nice full wine and perfect with venison and roast beef."

They all continued eating until William remarked, "Robbie was telling me this was the youngest dog's first shoot. You wouldn't have thought that."

"Which dog was that?" asked Charles.

"The one with the predominantly brown patches," William replied.

"She was exceptionally good at quartering. What energy," Charles said. "Thank you Lord Hugh. I haven't enjoyed myself so much for ages."

"Delighted to hear it," Lord Hugh responded and continued eating. When the roast beef was being served he addressed Charles and said, "Your father tells me you're studying law."

"Yes sir. I am."

"And whose pupillage are you under?"

"Adam Gillies sir. He's a good man. A good defence agent."

"Yes. I've heard quite a lot about him," Lord Hugh chortled. "As you know, Malcolm and William are on the other side. Malcolm was under William's pupillage for many years. Now they are colleagues and best friends, despite their occasional differences."

"Yes, we are good friends, father," his son responded. "But it's important to differ and of course there are always two sides to any story."

"Indeed there are," William stoically responded.

Amelia piped up and agreed. "Indeed there are. I've been reading a lot about the recent riots and the country seems to be quite divided at the moment."

"I thought you were spending your time painting Lady Amelia," said William affectionately to her.

"I have been recently," she retorted. "But before Charlotte arrived I was immersing myself in the daily news."

"It is important to keep abreast of what is happening," said her father.

"Towns are planting trees of liberty. And," she emphasised, "burning effigies of Dundas."

As soon as she said that, Malcolm started to smirk. "What's that face for Malcolm?" his father immediately asked

"Well. Dundas is such a pompous man. I find it quite amusing that people are burning his effigy."

"I am sure Dundas does not find amusing what's happening in France," his father sternly responded. "I read today that King Louis has been arrested and is being held in the Temple fortress. God knows, we don't want to have the masses rising up and overturning our monarchy."

"King George is a reasonable man," Amelia firmly stated. "They're just wanting voting reform. It seems a reasonable request."

"Well," William vehemently responded, "the action of the rioters could hardly be called … reasonable."

"Perhaps," Amelia conceded. "But they want their voices to be heard. Surely that is what democracy is all about."

"I quite agree with you my dear," her father benevolently said. "But let us lay politics aside and enjoy this delicious meal."

"I quite agree," Mr Macleod retorted. "It was a memorable shoot."

"You are all welcome to join us next year" Lord Hugh responded.

"And do say a heartfelt thanks to your gamekeeper" Mr MacLeod enthusiastically responded. "And congratulate him on his superbly trained dogs."

"I certainly will pass on the thanks," Lord Hugh earnestly replied. "We are very fortunate to have him." He paused. "Yes, Robbie is a very competent gamekeeper. And his son showed great promise so perhaps he will come back to the estate."

PART TWO

I

September was a turbulent month for Scotland's establishment. Friends of the People Societies were being formed in towns and cities throughout the land, all urging political reform. In England, Society members were almost exclusively aristocratic, but in Scotland, men of all classes were getting involved. The formation of so many societies caused great concern amongst politicians and other influential people who vehemently supported the status quo and were terrified the masses would rise and bring about a revolution as they did in France. By exaggerating the threat of the radicals to undermine reform proposals, Lord Henry Dundas, as Home Secretary, created powers to arrest any person suspected of wanting to change the form of government, or who was known to have sympathy for the French. He enhanced the network of spies who were ordered not only to report on the meetings – who was present, what was said – but also to report on private conversations. No-one was to be exempt from Government scrutiny. These draconian measures did not however stop the proliferation of pamphlets and handbills supporting Paine's stance on equal rights for all men appearing everywhere throughout cities and towns. Undeterred by the restraints on freedom of speech, these were surreptitiously printed and posted in public places stating:

"Those who have no votes for electing representatives are not free, as the rights of nature, as the principles of our constitution require, but are enslaved to the representation

116

of those who have votes. Citizens, we must rebel against the tyranny of power usurped."

The country became divided. One half wanted to retain the status quo, the other half to promote reform. Medals were made inscribing the political creed of each party: *"The Nation is essentially the source of all sovereignty."* or *"For a nation to be free it is sufficient it will it."* Towards the end of September, the Government became further alarmed when, on the twenty first of the month, the French National Assembly declared France to be a republic, abolished the monarchy and stripped King Louis of all his titles. He became Citizen Louis Capet. Then, to the great alarm of the ruling elites across the English Channel, the purge of all aristocrats started.

Meanwhile, around the same time in Edinburgh there was, in contrast, good news in the MacFadyen abode as John discovered one evening when he returned from work mid-evening. "John," Mrs MacFadyen excitedly exclaimed when he entered the kitchen. "Willie's jist arrived. He's back frae th' prison."

John immediately went over and clasped Willie's hand firmly. "Guid tae see ye. And ye Mrs MacPhail. Whit grand news!"

"Noo," Mrs MacFadyen said. "Sit yersels doon an' tell us a' aboot it."

Willie settled himself into a chair and smiled. "Tis grand tae be oot," and, putting his arm affectionately around his wife, "an' tae be wi' ma family again."

"Weel Mr MacPhail," responded his wife beaming at him with happiness, "we're gey glad ye're back. But how wis it?"

Willie retrieved his arm from behind his wife's back and, looking serious, said, "It wisnae that bad," He pondered for a bit then said, "It wis smelly, bit there were some guid yins there. An' whiles a body wid git a bottle o' whisky frae Mrs Laing's tavern doon th' stairs," he chortled. "She did a roarin' trade. An th'…"

Astonished Mr MacFadyen exclaimed, "Ye had a drink in prison!"

"Aye" Willie nonchalantly responded. "An' th' Peter didnae mind sae lang as he got a swig o't. Aye," he mused, "It may be a queer thing tae say, bit ah enjoyed sittin' on th' bench chattin' awa. Better that than thinkin' o' ma guidwife an' bairns wi'oot me at hame."

"An' whit a guidwife she is tae," added Mrs MacFadyen.

"Aye," he sombrely agreed, and, clasping his wife's hand, confessed, "It wisnae easy thinkin o' her working her fingers tae the bone, jist tae git food on the table."

"Aye." his wife quietly responded. "I hae tae be frank." She gave a deep sigh and continued. "It wis difficult in the early days, fur I had tae tell the customers. Ye wur away for sae lang, an' o' course customers were asking where ye wur. An' as soon as I telt them, they rushed awa." She paused. "Jist as I was aboot tae finish the last o' Willie's orders tho, thank God, mony o' the ladies an' gentlemen realised we wur the best glovers in the toon, an' they startit tae come back." She nodded her head pensively and added, "I think reluctantly. Bit," she straightened her back and continued, "we didnae starve." She smiled and looked at the MacFadyens. "Thanks tae our guid friends."

"An' you kept our reputation" Mr MacPhail proudly told his wife.

"Weel done!" Mrs MacFadyen pronounced emphatically.

"Aye," John heartily agreed. "Weel done."

"Bit," Mr MacFadyen responded in a serious tone, "were ye no lucky tae git oot?"

"Aye." Willie agreed. "An' I wis lucky no tae be chained, as mony o' the criminals wur in th' room. It wasnae guid fur th' spirit.....an' thon minister preachin' an' tellin' us we were a' sinners didnae help."

"Weel. You're oot o' it noo an' that's a' that maiters," said his wife, affectionately patting his hand."

"Bit, you'd better be careful," Mr MacFadyen warned, "fur Dundas is strengthening his grip on the Magistrates, gettin' them tae use a' the powers they hae tae arrest folk suspectit o' seditious acts." He looked at John. "You'd ken that lad. A' that typesetting at th' paper."

"Aye," John responded then lapsed into silence.

"Weel," Willie earnestly declared, "I hae nae intention o' ever getting' involved wi' onythin' ither than workin' an' lookin' efter the bairns an' guidwife." He paused. "It wisnae nice bein' cooped up in yon prison when I kennt ma krame wis richt ootdoors." Willie smiled sweetly at his wife. "But I'm awfy prood o' ma guidwife. We've still got the business." He smiled, "An' we'll be working th'gether agin."

"That's the spirit," his wife responded encouragingly. "We'll no dwell oan the past. Best tae forget it. Bit," she pondered, "goin' oot yon prison door an' straight tae ma stall ootside. That wasnae easy, bit," she perked up, "yer hame noo."

They all nodded in agreement.

Then Mr MacFadyen asked, "Did ye gang tae the Friendly Society?"

"Aye I did. Bit Willie wis in yon prison, an' they wudnae gie me a penny. Bit," and she looked affectionately at Mrs MacFadyen, "we were fortunate wi' oor neighbours. As I telt ye, ye an yer husband were wonderful." She paused momentarily then said, "An' thon neighbours in th' krames were guid. If I had tae git back tae th' bairns, there wis aye some body there tae bide th' stall. An' the neighbours here," she smiled sweetly at the MacFadyen's ," hae been wonderful. I hae been very fortunate". "An," she gripped her husband's arm with glee, "yer back hame."

Willie, addressing Mr and Mrs MacFadyen sombrely said, "Ah thank ye fur yer goodness towards oor family when I wis awa'. I'll no furget it."

"We wanted tae help as much as we coud. It wis a pleasure," Mrs MacFadyen pronounced.

"An' I dinnae want tae tak aboot politics an' a that," Willie said in a firm voice.

"Guid idea," Mr MacFadyen responded emphatically.

"Aye. We'll keep oor heids doon an' jist gie on wi' it," replied Willie with a sage smile.

He rose from his chair and, helping his wife out of hers, said, "Thank ye agin fir yur kindness. C'mon Mrs Macphail, lets git back tae th' bairns. They were asleep when I git back." He smiled, "I cannae wait tae see them in th' mornin'"

He took his wife's arm and as they were leaving Mrs MacFadyen called out gleefully, "It's sae guid tae see ye th'gither agin. And it will guid tae gang all th'gither tae the Kirk in the morning."

"Aye," said Mr MacPhail turning his head and beaming at her, "It's guid tae be back."

"Weel. Whit a grand surprise tae see Willie again," Mrs MacFadyen remarked as they closed the door.

"Aye," agreed her husband. "Indeed it wis."

"John. Ye'll be stervin'. Denner is aside th' hearth."

"Thanks Mrs MacFadyen. I am awfy hungry. It's been a long day."

"Ye were quiet this evening John," Mr MacFadyen observed as he relaxed back in his chair, his belly bursting over his breeches.

John, rising from his chair to step over to the stove to pick up his dinner, responded, "Aye. I'm exhausted. I'll hae an early night"

"Aye," replied Mr MacFadyen, "we huvnae seen ye fer ages."

" I've bin working other shifts as weel as ma ain. Bit Mr Brechin appreciates it and he's gaun tae gie me an oor aff on a Tuesday efternoon, fur a few weeks."

"That's guid o' him," Mr MacFadyen remarked.

"Aye. He's a guid man. I'm gaun tae Creech's tae treat masel' tae the Burns poetry book. I'm fair lookin' forward tae that."

"An' ye deserve it," said Mrs MacFadyen encouragingly. "Weel, husband. As soon as John hae finished, I'm gaun tae ma bed tae."

"I'll join ye then," responded his husband.

"Aye," said John. "a' I'm gaun tae so I can read ma book fur a while afore gaun tae sleep."

"Whit are ye reading?"

"Pilgrim's Progress," he smiled. "It taks ma mind aff things."

With that, he finished his meal, picked up a candle from the table, and bid them both goodnight.

II

Creech's Land, as it was known, was in a tenement block adjacent to St Giles, facing down the High Street. The front of the building commanded a view, on a clear day, right across to Aberlady Bay. The bookshop was on the first floor in a large room at the back. In a similar sized room at the front was a coffee shop where the literati of the town – lawyers, writers – would congregate to hear the latest gossip and news from Parliament House. It was a hubbub of intellectual activity.

As John walked up the dingy, narrow winding stone staircase to the entrance of the tenement, he anticipated with pleasure the atmosphere of the bookshop where shelves were laden with a vast array of books reaching almost to the ceiling. He had become a regular visitor over the past few weeks. It was a respite from typesetting reports of the turbulent times, and he had begun to think of the place as a sanctuary. A reader's delight, it was something to look forward to at the end of a hectic day.

The door to Creech's tenement was open, as it was from early in the morning till ten at night, and John crossed the hall into the spacious room which housed all the books. In the middle was a large table with a selection of the latest popular publications. Prominently displayed was Robert Burns book, '*Poems, Chiefly in the Scottish Dialect*'. Creech was a publisher, and Burns, who was keen to be published in Edinburgh, had asked him to publish the Kilmarnock edition, including other works he had written. Burns by this time had developed the reputation of being the 'Caledonian Bard' and was becoming a very popular person in Edinburgh society, so the copies of his works, including songs, were almost flying out of the door, enhancing Creech's financial assets.

John picked up a copy and as he was browsing through the index, looking for his favourite poem, '*A Cotter's Saturday night*', a voice behind him said, "Yer earlier the day John." He turned. It was Mr Creech, looking distinctive as ever, with his black silk breeches and powdered head.

"Aye. Mr Brechin has given me time off for a few weeks on a Tuesday so I thought I'd come here an'," he smiled, "instead o' just browsin', I'm gaun tae buy a copy o' the Burns."

"Guid choice," Mr Creech firmly stated and proudly announced, "I'm gaun tae be publishin' anither volume o' his whole new works. And," he continued enthusiastically, "he's writing a poem he thinks will be well received."

"What's it called?"

"*A Man's a Man for a' that*"."

"I look forward tae readin' it," John said as he handed over the six shillings for the copy. "I'll go an' sit in the coffee shop an' enjoy ma purchase."

"Aye lad," Mr Creech said, giving him an affectionate pat on the arm, "ye jist dae that."

Although the coffee room was busy there was a small, spare table nearby, and as he walked towards it he glanced round the room to see if he recognised Burns – he wasn't there – but he noticed two women seated at the table by the window. Judging by their attire he presumed it was a lady and her maid. The lady was reading a book whilst the maid was gazing out at the world beyond. Thinking nothing more about it, he sat down, opened the book and immediately became engrossed in the text, oblivious to his surroundings. Halfway through the poem, he heard distinctive female laughter. He turned his head to see where it was coming from, and there she was, sitting at the window. Amelia. What should he do? He felt scruffy in his work clothes, and apprehensive as to what to do. He glanced at her again. What elegance, he thought, admiring her outfit, her beige skirt with an olive green pelisse, complemented by a large turban shaped hat with stripes the same colours as her outfit. He gave a deep sigh and continued to deliberate. It was such a long time ago. Their lives had so changed since those days. She may not even remember him. But, he persuaded himself, go on, pluck up the courage and go over.

He picked up his book and bonnet and, clutching them in his hands, weaved his way amongst the busy tables and as he approached her called out, "Miss Amelia."

Amelia turned her head, looked at him momentarily. Then her expression altered to one of delighted recognition. "John," she exclaimed enthusiastically. "My goodness. After all this time. How are you?"

Standing bolt upright, clutching his book and bonnet he adjusted his accent and immediately responded, "Very well thank you, Miss Amelia."

"Oh. Don't be so formal," she humorously chastised him. "Meg," she animatedly addressed her maid. "This is John. His father is the gamekeeper on the estate. Do you remember me telling you of the times John and I spent together in the summer holidays?"

"Aye," Meg replied. "I do Madam."

"This is Meg, my maid, John." He nodded to her.

"It's lovely to see you after all this time," she said sincerely and, stretching out her hand, indicated a spare space at the table, "Do join us."

"Thank you," and feeling so much more relaxed, readily picked up a vacant nearby chair and sat beside her.

Amelia, on glancing at his book remarked, "Well John. I'm not surprised to see you in a bookshop after you persuading me to read all those summers ago."

"Aye," he responded, smiling, "it's one of my rare pleasures in life." Then he looked at her and burst into a wider smile. "Well Miss Amelia. I *am* surprised to see you in a bookshop. As far as I can recall, you were a reluctant reader."

She burst into a beautiful smile and laughed. "Yes. But times have changed."

Even though she said it in a frivolous fashion, John had a flash of realisation of how their lives had truly altered. "Aye," he quietly replied. "They have changed." But the hint of melancholy immediately disappeared when Amelia spoke and asked. "What's the book?"

He picked up his bonnet to retrieve the book and showed her the cover.

"Oh," she said, immediately interested. "Burns poetry."

"He's good. I can see why he's got the reputation of being the Caledonian Bard."

"I haven't yet read any of his works," she replied, kid gloved hands demurely clasped on her lap.

"But you. What are you reading?"

"Oh," she coquettishly responded, picking her book up from the table. "I don't think you'll approve."

"Why not?" he chuckled. "What is it?"

She glanced round, lowered her voice and said "It's Mary Wollstonecraft's new book …"

"The Vindication of the Rights of Women," he interjected.

"You know of it?"

"Aye. I've read a few reviews." He smiled. "I shouldn't think Miss Pringle would have recommended it."

"Indeed not. Actually, I've just received the copy today and have only read a few pages. Mr Creech ordered it for me and I picked it up when we arrived." She smiled at Meg. "It was John who introduced me to reading, much to my father's delight."

"Aye he was pleased I encouraged you." Pausing for a moment he wistfully remarked, "It was a long time ago."

"Yes," she mused, "Those were happy days indeed. Gosh. To think we were friends for years when we were young and it's already been five years since you came to the city. How do you like it?"

He pondered. "It took a while to adjust. I miss country life."

"Me too, I suppose, but I go back to the estate every summer."

"Aye. I was visiting my parents for a week in the summer and was recalling those days…"

"You should have come to visit," she gently chastised him.

"Well," said John, remembering the last time he did see her, "I was helping my father."

"Next time," she firmly told him, "you must come."

"Thank you." Then, thinking of her riding, asked, "Do you still have Christie?"

"Yes. I had a friend staying and we rode every morning."

John looked at Meg, smiled, and said, "She was a wild rider. Reckless at times going through the forest."

"And so were you!" she laughed.

"Maybe I was," he smiled. "But it was good fun."

"It certainly was. And how is the job? Are you still with the *Caledonian Mercury*?"

"Aye. Still at the same job. It's all right."

"Well, you never know, when your father retires you might be tempted to come back to the estate."

"Maybe," he chuckled. "But he won't be retiring for a while. He's very fit."

"Yes. He exercises the dogs every day."

"Aye. He loves those animals. How were they on the shoot this year?"

"I wasn't on it, but judging from the comments we heard when they came back, he seems to have done a great job with the dogs."

"That is good to hear." He paused, sighed and said, "I do miss open spaces. Particularly as we're comin' into the winter and all the smoke. But," he said, brightening up "most of the time, I feel fine being here. When did you get to the city?" he asked.

"We came last autumn. I'm enjoying the change and I'm making new friends." She looked at him affectionately. "You were the only friend I had when I was young, but," perking up added, "I'm making up for it now."

"That's good. It's important to have friends." He had just finished speaking when he heard the clock at St Giles strike three. "I have to get back to work. I don't usually have time off during the day but I've been working long shifts and I've been given an hour off on a Tuesday for a while."

"Well," Amelia enthusiastically responded, "let's meet here next Tuesday at two. It's so nice to see you again."

"Indeed it is," he replied sincerely and rose from his chair to bid them goodbye: "See you next week. And enjoy your book. I look forward to hearing your views on it."

"Yes," she smiled. "It'll be interesting to see if the reviews are accurate. Probably not." She tittered. "They're all from a male perspective."

He smiled at her. "We're not all so dogmatic."

She laughed. "See you next week John."

He bade them both goodbye and, as he left the coffee shop and was scampering down the stairs, he realised he hadn't felt so elated for a very long time.

III

That evening Amelia was going with her father to the opening concert of the St Cecilia's Hall season. She felt in a frivolous mood as she and Meg were choosing her attire for the evening. Having browsed the collection, they both agreed she would look elegant in the full length brocaded cream dress. Amelia had a slim, lithe figure and the design of the dress accentuated her slender waist. Meg expertly rolled up her golden locks, leaving a ringlet on either side, and secured them with a ruby stone clasp. Her earrings matched the clasp and her two strand necklace consisted of beautiful gold filigree work. Unlike many young ladies of the day, Amelia chose not to paint her face, preferring a natural look. "You look as pretty as a picture M'am," commented Meg.

Being the first concert of the season, the foyer of St Cecilia's Hall was packed with guests when they arrived all engaged in animated conversation. Amelia and her father greeted several people, then made their way up the left-hand side of the double staircase which led to the concert hall on the first floor.

As they were settling down, Mr Thornton, the proprietor of the musical society, came onto the stage. "Please take your seats Ladies and Gentlemen. The concert is about to begin."

When everyone was eventually seated, amidst much hustle and bustle, Mr Thornton began. "It is a rare pleasure to see you all at this our first concert of the season. I hope you will approve of the programme. I certainly do." The audience tittered as he did. "And we have the rare pleasure of telling you that you will be the first to hear a collaboration I have been involved with our Caledonian Bard. Robert Burns is collaborating with me to create the 'The Melodie of Scotland' which will be performed at some point during the season. But back to tonight, we are delighted to welcome on stage the Guiseppi Quartet who will be performing two of my favourite compositions - Hadyn's String Quartet number forty-nine in B minor and his quartet number fifty-three in D major." He smiled at the audience then retired as the musicians came onto the stage.

Half way through the first movement, Amelia began to think of the meeting with John. What a pleasure to meet up again with someone who knew her as she was in her tomboy, petulant youth. And, as music permeated the hall, she started to reminisce about those special, carefree days and the adventures she and John had engaged in. It truly was a happy time for her. But, she smartly reminded herself, glancing round at the wealthy patrons, her life had dramatically changed from that of her youth. She was a part of the elite, and that was how it would always be.

The first performance finished. The audience gave the quartet a rapturous response and the interval began. She and her father left their seats – he going to friends – she to Charlotte whom she saw in the distance. But as she was bustling through the crowd she heard a voice call out, "Amelia." She turned. It was William. Handsome as ever, she thought. He looked quite distinguished in his Advocate's black gowned outfit, with his starched white shirt and white cravat.

"Oh," Amelia remarked, "I didn't see you when I arrived."

He was obviously delighted to see her and animatedly responded, "I was working late. I came in just as the concert was about to begin and sat at the back. I didn't want to miss the first of the season."

"Yes," Amelia enthused. "They're wonderful players."

"And you too have a wonderful gift for the piano," he told her encouragingly. "You should give a recital here."

"Thank you William," she smiled. "Perhaps I will one day."

"I hope so," he jovially responded. "And what have you been doing since you returned to the city?"

"Oh. Just the usual," she flippantly replied. "Playing the piano, painting. Reading."

"What are you reading?"

She decided to be forthright. "Actually, I've been reading the Mary Wollstonecraft book and reports about the insurrections. I don't know why the militia are being brought in. It's completely unnecessary. The Societies are bound to peaceful protests…"

"I'm not so sure about that," William firmly interjected. "There are some dangerous people involved in them. And," he continued in an exasperated tone "I really don't think you should be bothering about these issues. It'll all be over soon enough."

"How can you be so sure?

"I'll tell you another time. Oh," he saw Lord Hugh and beckoned him over. "Hello sir. How are you this evening?"

"Very well indeed," responded Lord Hugh. "And what have you two been discussing?"

William grinned, "Amelia's piano skills. I was suggesting she should give a concert here."

"What an encouraging idea William. You must join us for dinner soon. It's always a pleasure to have your company."

"And mine too sir," he smiled at Amelia.

Just then Mr Thornton came onto the stage to announce that the second half would begin and would the audience please take their seats.

"We'll arrange a date," Lord Hugh told William as they started to make their way back to their seats.

"Yes sir that would be good."

Once seated Lord Hugh turned to his daughter and remarked. "What a nice chap that William is. Don't you think Amelia?"

"Yes father. He is."

When the second half began William's mind started to drift. He thought Amelia looked enchanting. She really was a rather beautiful woman, and spirited. He admired that, but she would have to be kept in her place. He continued musing. She had all the accoutrements of a wife and he was at a marriageable age and of course he had prospects, being very well thought of at the bar. "Yes," he mused, "She would make a very good wife. With very good connections."

The concert ended and, when the enthusiastic clapping had subsided. William heard his name being called. He turned. It was his friend Thomas in a nearby row. "Are you going to the club?"

"Indeed I am," William heartily responded. They arranged to rendezvous in the foyer but before he had a chance to say goodbye to Amelia, Thomas had already set off.

It was the custom after a concert for the directors and friends to go to Fortune's Tavern to drink a few bottles of claret and have a snack of oysters. Held in a room upstairs, when they arrived, several bottles of claret were already placed on a table, including a vast decanter of fortified wine. This was to be drunk in bumpers when the traditional oratorio was sung in praise of the various beauties who were at the concert that evening. As they downed their glasses toasting the various women, William was tempted to tell his friend which beauty he had toasted but thought it auspicious to wait for a more opportune moment. After the toasting, anecdotes were related about particular judges recently disgracing themselves in a drunken state, but being perfectly capable of sitting on the bench the following day and making articulate judgements. By the time he and Thomas left, they too were in a drunken state but, as he was lurching up the hill to his lodgings in Byres Close he chose that evening to ignore the enticing lewd comments from prostitutes beckoning him to sample their trade in the comfort of one of the many burgeoning brothels in the city, and focused entirely on Amelia. He stumbled a little way. Then he stopped. Straightened his back, attempted to sober up, and recalled the vision he had had in the chapel on the estate, the day after the shoot. When the sermon began, he had a flash of an image of he and Amelia being married in that very place. Recent events had put that image to the back of his mind, but now it had been resurrected. "Yes! "he shouted out in his drunken state. "I shall have her as my wife."

IV

When Amelia retired that evening, snuggled up in her already warmed comfortable four poster bed, she started to read Mary Wollstonecraft's book. After the first few pages she became engrossed with her analytical comments about the role of middle class women in society, and how their only education was to please men and gain a wealthy husband. After reading for a considerable time she stopped, laid the book on the coverlet, sat up, plumped up her pillows and started to contemplate her own upbringing.

She had been brought up by her governess, Miss Pringle, and her father, to believe her purpose in life was to become a lady. Amelia took it for granted that she and Malcolm had a different education. While Miss Pringle immersed her in Shakespeare's plays and poetry, her brother was tutored by Mr Brown in Latin, Greek, Algebra and history. And of course, leading such a sheltered life, she had no idea how other girls were educated. She took it for granted her goal was to become accomplished in various pursuits – playing the piano, needlework and the like. Although, she had so enjoyed her carefree childhood summers with John and it took her a while to get over the loss of his company each time they were parted, life had continued along her maiden-like path. Until recently.

William's dismissal of her curiosity in political affairs had prompted her to start reading the papers and immerse herself in life outside of her own, and those of her circle. Her father had always encouraged her to have an enquiring mind but if she hadn't been so offended by William's comment she might have been satisfied with the bland subjects the ladies in the art club discussed each week: who did what; where they went; whom they met; what new dresses they had acquired; who was cheating at cards. Politics were never mentioned in her circle. However, she was going to attempt to change that. She had been appalled at Malcolm's descriptions of the conditions slaves were being kept in and, having read more about the issue, she decided to join the women's Abolition Society. Josiah Wedgwood, one of the founding members of the Society for the Abolition of the Slave Trade, asked his sculptor to create an image representing the plight of black slaves. The image was put on many accessories, including a cameo, which Amelia ordered with money from her allowance, knowing her father would approve.

When the cameo arrived with the post, the parcel included an extract from a poem the abolitionist Hannah More had written describing the turmoil of an enslaved woman, wrenched from her children.

> *"I see, by more than Fancy's mirrow shewn,*
> *The burning village, and the blazing town:*
> *See the dire victim torn from social life,*
> *The shrieking babe, the agonizing wife!*
> *She, wretch forlorn! is dragg'd by hostile hands,*
> *To distant tyrants sold, in distant lands!*
> *Transmitted miseries, and successive chains,*
> *The sole sad heritage her child obtains!*
> *Ev'n this last wretched boon their foes deny,*
> *To weep together, or together die.*
> *By felon hands, by one relentless stroke,*
> *See the fond links of feeling nature broke!*
> *The fibres twisting round a parent's heart,*
> *Torn from their grasp, and bleeding as they part.*
> *Hold, murderers, hold! not aggravate distress;*
> *Respect the passions you yourselves possess;"*

Amelia had opened the parcel in her bedchamber while she was sitting at her dressing table. After she had read it she thought what a wretched life some people led. And – glancing round at her room she noted, for the first time, her opulent environment. The luxuriant, burgundy velvet drapes; the dainty walnut engraved commode with the delicate brass handles; the fire in the grate (lit by the housemaid); her mahogany kneehole dressing table and the huge, hand-woven, Turkish rug. What a privileged life she led surrounded by wealth, comfort, and security. But, she resolved, she would do all she could to raise awareness of the hardships, grief and pain these enslaved women had to endure because as William had said 'it is good for the economy'. She would take the poem to her art class, read it at the break, and hopefully encourage more women to get involved in the Abolition Movement and persuade them to purchase one of the accessories. Then, she would suggest they read Wollstonecraft's book. Animated, she finally felt she had a purpose in life, and could not wait to tell John.

On the day of their next meeting John decided to wear his best coat, the one he wore for the Sabbath. He wanted to look more presentable and, in his green calf length woollen threaded coat with a large, round collar, he did. He left his lodgings early so Mrs MacFadyen wouldn't query him as to why he was wearing it. James of course was curious as to why he had brought the coat to work. John though had no intention of telling him.

John left for the coffee house slightly before the time they had arranged to meet and, when he entered the busy room, saw the table at the window was free. He quickly poured himself a cup of coffee popping his penny in the bowl, strode over to the table, pulled up another chair nearby, sat down and waited for Amelia to arrive. When he saw her coming in the door with Meg, he stood up and waved over to her. She saw him, gave a welcoming smile and, as Meg was getting the coffee, went over to him.

"Have you had a good week?" he asked as they sat down.

"It's been very productive," she mischievously responded.

He chuckled. "So what have you been doing?"

"Well," she began, as Meg joined them with the coffees. "Sit down Meg. I'm just about to tell John about my week. Meg knows all about it, so why don't you change chairs. Meg can sit at the window and we can talk."

Once they had swopped seats she leant forward and, in a hushed tone, said, "Two things have happened." She paused. "I've joined the Women's Abolition Society..."

"What a good idea," he replied, also in a hushed voice. "I've been typesetting many harrowing accounts of how slaves are treated. It isn't right."

"No. It is not," she firmly agreed. "I ordered a Wedgwood anti-slavery cameo." She put a hand to her neck to show him the cameo which was pinned to a cerise velvet band. "What do you think?"

John bent slightly forward to look at it. It was an arresting image. Set against a white background was a raised relief figure of a muscular black man kneeling, with his wrists and ankles enchained. Naked, but for a loin cloth, his head was held high. His arms were outstretched and his hands were clasped together as if beseeching the universe to recognise his plight.

"It's a shocking image," John sombrely responded

"Yes," she lowered her eyes and, in a soft voice, said, "it is."

"What does the inscription say at the top? I couldn't read it."

She solemnly replied, "Am I not a Man and a Brother?. The motto is the seal of the Abolition Society."

John sighed. "What a life."

They sat in silence for a moment then Amelia perked up. "Josiah Wedgwood is a fervent abolitionist," she enthusiastically told him. "He's a wonderful man. He's used the image on accessories – bracelets, brooches, hair-pins, necklaces." She chuckled. "He even has the image inlaid in gold on men's snuffboxes ....and crockery."

"Good for him."

"It's important for us all to get involved in such a good cause." She leant towards him, and in a hushed tone said, "John. I can't tell you how good it makes me feel to do something with my life to help people."

"You've always been kind-hearted." He smiled at her, and as he did so she noticed the scar beside his right eye, and remembered their gallops in the forest the last summer they spent together and how one day a branch had slapped his face and given him a horrible cut. They had immediately ridden back and Mrs MacPherson applied her medicinal remedies and skill and the cut healed remark-ably quickly, leaving only a small scar. She smiled at the thought of it.

John, misinterpreting the smile, smiled back. "Are you remembering you weren't always kind-hearted?"

She laughed. "Well. As of now I am transforming into a better person." Her expression altered and she became serious. "I bought the cameo because I thought the image would be seen better than on a bracelet or a hair pin. And by wearing it I hope it'll be noticed and encourage more people to contemplate the plight of slaves."

"That's a noble gesture to make," he declared.

"Have you joined?" she asked.

"Well," he hesitated, "Mr Brechin has made it quite plain he doesn't want any of the staff to be involved in politics."

"But," she indignantly responded, "wanting abolition of the slave trade isn't politics. It's justice."

"I know it is," he sternly replied. "But I have to think of my job."

"But you should think beyond that." She paused. "You have to look to your conscience."

Furious, he hissed, "Of course I've got a conscience. But I have to prioritise my life. I can't sign a petition if I think I might lose my job."

"But there are other papers you could work for…"

"Aye. But I'd need a reference. And with everything going on at the moment, there's not going to be anybody employing a person who's involved in politics."

Oh," she sounded disappointed. "That means you're not going to join the movement?" She lowered her eyes. "If I were a man, I would."

John responded in an agitated tone, whispering, "I told you. I've got my job to think about."

"But John," she earnestly looked at him. "You could get another job. Go back to the country. Follow in your father's footsteps. Become a gamekeeper." She gave a deep sigh. "Nothing will change unless people protest against these injustices." She looked at him earnestly.

"If every man hesitated to become a member of the societies, no momentum would ever gather. Just think. You could be contributing to the emancipation of men. It's a wonderful cause."

"I can see that" he replied in a sombre tone.

"I do *not* want to pressure you, but will you at least think about it?"

He gave a deep sigh and soberly responded, "I will."

Just then the chimes of the St Giles clock nearby struck three quarters to the hour. "Well, just before you go," said Amelia brightening up, "the second thing that's exciting is that I've been immersing myself in the Mary Wollstonecraft book. I'd read a few reviews before I bought it. They were all male writers and scathing in their comments." She elevated her posture and smiled: "It was an encouragement to purchase the book."

"Quite right."

"Oh! I thought you would be like all other males and repudiate her arguments."

"Which one?"

She looked at him earnestly, "That women are accoutrements of men - nothing more, nothing less." She shrugged her shoulders. "And that's what my education was for. To ensure I would make," she smiled at him. "and I know this bit by heart… 'an advantageous match and ultimately become a pliable wife.'" Her expression changed immediately to one of distaste. "I could think of nothing worse."

John burst out in raucous laughter and spluttered, "No. I could think of nothing worse for you either." Then Amelia spontaneously joined him in laughing heartily. Meg, witnessing their joviality, was very surprised at her mistress's response. She had only ever seen her mistress being restrained in male company, but was glad she looked happy.

Amelia leaned towards John and said, "Listen to this." She retrieved a piece of paper from the beautiful, hand embroidered reticule which was on her lap and animatedly told him, "I was riveted when I read this passage in the book," before reciting: "'To rise in the world, and have the liberty of running from pleasure to pleasure, they must marry advantageously, and to this object their time is sacrificed, and their persons often legally prostituted.'." She paused. "Well," she said indignantly, "I want to put my education to better use."

"Quite right." He smiled affectionately at her, "You must never lose your spirit." Then, remembering the time, he stood up and said, "I've got to go."

"Will you be here next week?"

"No. I've got to work that day. But," he smiled, "I could be here in two weeks' time."

"That would be very nice. See you then," then added, "It's so nice we are rekindling our friendship."

Delighted John responded, "Aye. It is." And bidding them both goodbye he dashed off to his work.

V

A few days later the cold chill of autumn and a penetrating wind greeted John as he stepped onto the High Street after his shift. The haze from the smoke of lit fires in the densely populated city with its packed towering tenements was being dispersed by the wind as John began to walk down the street to his lodgings. Darkness had descended and a lamplighter had already lit several lanterns on the High Street. As John viewed him in the distance, carrying his ladder and accompanied by a young lad carrying a jug of oil, he almost trod on a cat scavenging in the cobbles. To avoid it, he stepped aside and accidentally bumped into a burly man walking in the opposite direction. Mumbling apologies, John was just about to set off again when the man called out, "Hello there. How are ye?" John turned, looked at the face in the dim light and realised it was the man in Fortune's Tavern. The person he had been avoiding since the encounter.

"Whit are ye doin' th' nicht?" he asked.

John was going to say he was meeting a friend but Peter had had to cancel and, being an honest person, he spontaneously replied, "Nithin' much."

"Weel," responded the man, "I'm jist aff tae a meetin' at Lawrie's Rooms in the Lawnmarket. Why no' come alang?"

"Oh," John hesitated. "I'm no sure aboot that."

"C'mon lad," the man urged. "It'll be short."

John hesitated remembering Amelia's disappointment at his lack of involvement in the movement and changed his mind. "A' right, jist the once."

"Guid lad," the man responded and they started to walk briskly up the hill in the direction of the Lawnmarket. When they passed Old Fishmarket Close, John put his head down in case he was seen by any of his colleagues, but there was nobody around at that time of night. They walked in silence for a while then the man said, "I'm Donald by the way. Whit's yer name?"

"John."

"An'whit dae ye dae?" asked Donald.

John was reluctant to tell him in case Mr Brechin found out, but as he was only going to this one meeting he replied. "I'm a typesetter."

"Workin' on the papers?" Donald queried.

"Aye."

"Weel," Donald positively responded, "ye'll ken whit's happening in a' the cities."

"Aye," John agreed. "There's been a lot o' publicity aboot the societies."

"Quite right too," remarked Donald. "I cannae see how the Government can ignore the wishes o' the people."

"We'll see," John earnestly responded. They continued in silence until they reached their destination.

Upstairs in Lawrie's Rooms, they could hear the din of animated voices as they approached the door. "It's busy richt enough," Donald remarked as they entered a room packed with working men of all ages. Donald immediately shook hands with a man nearby. "Guid tae see ye agin Mac," he said, shaking the man's hand vigorously. "An' I brought John." John nodded to the man.

"Are ye a new member?" the man asked.

"Na," John firmly responded. "Jist a visit."

"Weel, nae maiter," the man pleasantly responded. "Ye'll always be welcome."

John glanced round the room. With a roaring fire in the grate, and friendly voices, there was indeed a convivial atmosphere. Two men, clutching a bundle of papers in their arms, approached a table at the far end of the room and placed their notes down in front of them. One of them picked up a gavel, which was already on the table, and struck it once. "Gentlemen," he announced. "Please take your seats, or stand if you have to, and the meeting will commence." Much shuffling could be heard before the group settled down and then bent their heads. "Dear Lord," the organiser spoke. "We ask thee to bless this meeting and all those who attend. Amen." Amen was echoed round the room. "Now, my colleague Mr MacDairmid will introduce the meeting by calling out motions which Captain Johnston has put forward."

A stout, middle aged man in the front row stood up and addressed the members. He had distinguished curly ginger whiskers. "I hope ye'll agree tae these motions fellow members. It's a' in a guid cause." He sat down.

"Thank ye Captain Johnston," said Mr MacDairmid and, in an authoritative voice, proceeded to read from a piece of paper. "The motions proposed by our member are first: 'That the names of any person or person, belonging to the Associated Friends of the People, who may be found guilty of rioting, or creating or aiding sedition or tumult, shall be expunged from the books of the society.' The second motion is that 'any person acting properly who may be persecuted or oppressed by the arm of power, shall be protected by the whole societies.' Those Members, are the motions we wish to be passed into resolutions at our next meeting.

I would also like to remind you that the first edition of Captain Johnston's weekly newspaper the *Edinburgh Gazettee*r will be published this Friday. Now," he placed the paper back on the table and picked up another. "As ye ken, we always hae readings from Paine's works an' I'll no alter that part o' the proceedings as we are a' gathered here tae urge the Government tae give us voting rights. So Gentlemen, Paine writes: 'Rouse then, ye Britons! Awake from the slumbering state of apathy in which you have so long suffered yourselves ingloriously to remain! Open your eyes to the injuries which have been heaped on you; and assert your right to have them redressed. Evince to all the world that you are the true descendants and sons of your once famed glorious ancestors; prove yourselves worthy to inherit, in its highest degree of perfection, that constitution, which they raised by their valour, and cemented with their blood. Raise your voice – the voice of the people – and sound in the ears of tyrants and their abettors, that you will be free and you are so: that voice is the noble, the mighty fiat, which none can, or dare to, attempt to gainsay.'" He paused to pick up another piece of paper. "And this ye are tae contemplate." He cleared his throat and in a clear voice started to recite slowly. "'Those who have no votes for electing representative are not free, as the rights of nature, and the principles of our constitution require, but are enslaved to the representative of those who have votes.' A very powerful message members! And anither passage: 'A government where the executive and legislative power meet in a single person has no more pretence to freedom: it is perfect despotism; and the people who submit to it are in a state of slavery …'."

John stopped listening because he immediately remembered his father reciting that very quote and how angry his father had become when John mentioned Dundas' power over the Magistrates. He was horrified at that power and thought that was despotism. John looked round at the men in the room. Apart from one man in the corner taking notes, they were all listening attentively, periodically nodding their heads in agreement to words being spoken from the quotes. John wasn't sure if he felt comfortable in the environment. He had been adamant for months about his non-involvement stance, but maybe he should not be so rigid. Maybe he should step out of his insular life and get involved in a real cause. But… what would he do about work? Maybe he could go back to the land. Maybe, he should not do anything. But he wondered what Amelia might think of him joining. He smiled to himself and thought she would probably be proud of him, but … that wouldn't pay the bills. He realised she was now constantly in his thoughts but if he joined the movement that would give him something else to think about.

Mr MacDairmid stopped speaking and sat down. His colleague then stood up and announced: "Members. I thank ye all for coming this evening. Before we adjourn, the committee propose that at the next meeting we elect Thomas Muir of Huntershill to be Vice-President of the Friends of the People Society." He paused then said, "Thank you for coming this evening and we look forward to seeing you all again at the next meeting on the twenty eighth of November. In the meantime, hold dear to the cause and I wish you all well."

The room had been engulfed in silence since the start of the meeting but now it burst into animated discussions amongst the men. Donald turned to John and asked, "Are ye comin' tae the White Hart Inn?"

Still hesitant about getting involved, he mumbled, "I dinnae think sae."

"C'mon lad," Donald immediately responded. "Dinnae be shy. They're a guid bunch o' folk."

It was true, John thought, there really was a convivial atmosphere in the room. There would be no harm done going for a drink with them. Just the once, he reminded himself. "Aye," he replied. "I will come."

"Guid lad," Donald jovially retorted, then turned to Mac, "Are ye comin' tae the White Hart fur a dram?"

"Oh aye," Mac responded enthusiastically. The door was opened and men started to pour out of the room down the stairs. Donald beckoned some other men to join them and they set off down to the Grassmarket. En route, one of Donald's acquaintances walked alongside John. "My name's Alec. Whit's yers?"

"John."

"Guid tae meet ye John. It's grand ye're joining us."

"I dinnae ken if I am," said John, thinking of Willie. "Whit aboot gettin' arrested?"

"Och," Alec nonchalantly retorted. "I shouldn't think aboot that. There are tae mony o' us tae git arrested."

"Maybe," John ponderously replied.

"Dundas has his agents at the meetings," Alec continued. "Bit we just want tae spread the message aboot wanting reform. That's all. So the government hae nothin' tae worry aboot," Alec said, sounding perky, "I'm lookin' forward tae ma pint o' ale an' ye look like ye are tae."

"Aye," John smiled. "I am."

When they arrived at the Inn it was packed with bodies. "Looks like we winnae git served," said John.

"Aye we will," Alec replied. "We've a room at the back. Donald is a friend o' the landlord an' he aye makes sure there's space fur us. C'mon. Follow me."

They weaved their way amongst the busy tables. At the back was a corridor with a small room off to the right. "Here we are," said Alec. "I'll juist go 'n' git the wench. Settle in," he told John, pointing to a nearby chair.

Donald and the other men arrived, full of the talk of the meeting. When Alec came back he was followed by the wench carrying a tray full of jugs of ale. Alec took a couple off the tray, sat down beside John, took a sip and said, "Aye. That's guid. I've got a terrible thirst on me the nicht." They sat silently for a few minutes while they sipped and savoured the taste of the ale then Alec spoke. "It's guid they're proposing Thomas Muir as Vice-President. He's daein' a lot fur the cause. Donald is friendly wi' the coach drivers who work the Stirling and Glasgow routes an' they've been telling him that Muir is travelling aroond spreading the word an' getting meetings set up."

"Aye. He's a guid man," agreed John. "I covered the Bertram trial. Muir did a grand job defending him but there wis nae justice wi' the verdict."

"I remember it. So, whit is it ye dae? Are ye a lawyer?"

"Na. I'm a typesetter on the *Caledonian Mercury*. I did the transcript o' the trial…"

"Oh," Alec was impressed. "So ye'll ken a' aboot the political situation an' that."

"Aye. We typeset reports every day. 'An' you? Whit dae ye dae?"

"I'm a printer." Interested, John asked where. "At Peter Williamson's. The book seller."

"Whit dae ye publish?"

"Popular novels an' the like," Alec told him adding: "We could dae wi a guid typesetter."

"Well. I'm happy where I am," said John and not wanting to engage any further in that conversation he began to drink quickly and soon finished his pint.

"Wud ye like anither?"

"Na thanks," John replied as he stood up and started to leave.

"It wis guid tae meet ye. An' if ye'd like tae visit the print room it's in Robertson Close in the Cowgate," and he added. "I'm usually workin' in the evenings."

"Thanks fur the invitation. I'll think aboot it." He called goodbye to Donald and left hasitily, but instead of walking up West Bow to the High Street, he decided to continue on to the Cowgate and have a glimpse at Peter's print room in Robertson Close. Despite the light from the street lamps, the Cowgate was a dingy part of the city with its numerous narrow dark alleys where some of the poorest lived in hovels. But there was little crime in the area as the streets were regularly patrolled by the Town Guards.

He finally reached his destination and turned into the dark close at the far end of the Cowgate. When he entered it, the stench of excrement was almost overwhelming as the cobbled close was seldom sluiced. It was in a squalid part of the city where large families lived in single rooms in abject poverty, eking out an existence on whatever way they could. The tall tenement blocks were crammed together on either side of closes, the narrow passageways which never saw the light of day. Looking up at the tenements in the close he caught the occasional glimmer of candle light filtering through small gaps in the shutters. There was though one tenement, halfway up on the right hand side, where the ground floor room was in complete darkness. No sign was attached to the door but John presumed this was Alec's print room. He also thought that the anonymity of the place would be perfect for printing the so-called seditious pamphlets and handbills being distributed throughout the town. Having satisfied his curiosity as to where Alec worked, he turned and left. Not wanting to dally or be beckoned by numerous ladies of the night, he smartened his step, careful to avoid the rotting rubbish strewn on the street, and walked briskly up St Mary's Wynd back to his lodgings, unsure in which direction his life should take him.

VI

Before John and Amelia's next meeting, her father had organised a soiree. He had invited William, his country neighbour Mr McLeod and his son, Charles. Amelia's friendship with Charlotte had started to blossom when she discovered Charlotte was a flautist. They had been rehearsing one of Mozart's flute and piano sonatas for this evening. Mozart was a virtuoso pianist and the sonatas were composed primarily for he and his sister, who was a flautist. You had to have exceptionally nimble fingers to play the piece as the runs in the first and final movements were complex. Mozart's sister was also an accomplished flautist so the piece did require a lot of rehearsal. Charlotte and Amelia however thoroughly enjoyed themselves practising the sonata they had chosen and had spent many hours preparing for this evening.

Amelia, Charlotte and Malcolm were already in the drawing room, standing beside the roaring fire in the ornate cast iron grate when the guests arrived punctually at seven thirty. William was the first to come into the room. He waved to Malcolm and strode over to join them.

"How lovely to see you Amelia," he greeted her. "And may I say how enchanting you look tonight."

"Thank you William," she pleasantly responded. "You remember my friend Miss Charlotte?"

"Of course I do," he replied, nodding his head in acknowledgement and adding: "A pleasure to see you again." He then turned his attention to Amelia and asked, "And what piece have you chosen for our pleasure this evening?"

Amelia glanced at Charlotte then back to William. "We're playing a Mozart flute and piano sonata,"

"Oh," William spontaneously replied, "one of my favourite composers."

Her father entered the room before she was able to respond and called out, "Come and welcome Mr McLeod and Charles, my dear." She smiled at William and, as she glided over to greet them, William turned to Charlotte and asked, "Have you been playing the flute for long?"

"Two years," she responded. "I love the instrument. And of course it's portable so it has been no problem to rehearse with Amelia." She smiled demurely at William. "We had fun rehearsing."

"Delighted to hear that," he replied. "I'm looking forward to the recital."

"Oh. That sounds very formal," adding, "We're not professional players, but we enjoy playing duets."

Amelia, having joined the newcomers, cordially addressed them. "How nice to see you again."

"Indeed it is Miss Amelia." Full of bonhomie Mr McLeod continued, "And we are so looking forward to hearing you and Miss Charlotte play."

Feeling a little nervous, Amelia responded, "Well, Miss Charlotte and I have been practising for a while. Hopefully we won't make too many mistakes," and smiled magnanimously at them.

"Come," said Lord Hugh. "Sit down. Make yourselves comfortable." And, hearing Benjamin enter the room with a tray of full glasses, turned and said "Benjamin, could you pass a glass of claret to the guests."

"Certainly m'lud."

The men were served a drink and sat down.

"Well my dear," Lord Hugh said to his daughter. "Shall we begin?"

"Yes father." As she was walking over to the piano she picked up a large candlelit candelabra from a nearby table and placed it on the piano so they both could read the music. While Amelia was settling herself on the piano stool, Charlotte picked up her flute and the music stand beside her and went to join Amelia. She adjusted the music on her stand, waited for Amelia to count the beats in, and began.

As William watched Amelia's dexterous fingers weave up and down the keyboard he envisaged them having similar soirees when they were married. Perhaps not in such an opulent environment as Lord Hugh's drawing room which looked magnificent, with beautiful pictures adorning the walls, lit candelabras on tables and walls, and a candlelit crystal chandelier which looked nothing less than magnificent. Still, he would do his best to provide her with as much comfort as possible. And then he thought how privileged he was to be so close to this family, and how fortunate he had been to take Malcolm under his wing. And, as he listened to the beautiful refrain in the slow movement, it occurred to him that the Caledonian Hunt Ball, being held next month, would be an auspicious time to ask Amelia for her hand. Malcolm had once told him the romantic story of his father proposing to his mother at a ball, and he thought Lord Hugh would appreciate his future son-in-law doing the same. He continued ruminating on life with Amelia until the sonata finished. When it did, they all clapped enthusiastically in appreciation of their performance.

"Well done!" exclaimed Mr McLeod. "What talented musicians you are."

"Indeed they are," agreed Lord Hugh. "Well done Amelia and Charlotte. It was a delightful recital and there were no mistakes my dear. All that rehearsing was worth it."

"We loved doing it. And," she smiled, "we could be tempted to practise another sonata for another time."

"That would be marvellous," said William. "Your playing is very impressive. It was most enjoyable."

"Indeed it was," echoed Lord Hugh. "Benjamin, could you refill our glasses?"

"Certainly m'lud." And, as soon as he had refilled the glasses, he retired.

"Did it take you long to learn the piece?" asked Mr McLeod.

"Not too long," Amelia replied. "We practised for about a week, but we had both been learning our own parts for a while. And it is such a pleasure to play with Charlotte," she said, smiling to her friend. "And I love the flute, and of course the piano."

"Do you play frequently?" he asked.

"Yes, every day if I possibly can. It gives me a great deal of pleasure. And of course we bought this grand piano recently. It's a beautiful instrument to play. It's got a lovely touch."

"Yes," Lord Hugh replied, "we were very excited when it was delivered. Amelia assures me it lives up to its expectations."

"I thought you played beautifully," said William, hastily adding, "and so did you Miss Charlotte. It was a delightful recital."

"It was indeed," mirrored Malcolm. "Well done to you both."

"Do any of your family play an instrument Mr McLeod?" asked Lord Hugh.

"Sadly no. They don't. Although Charles did think of taking up the violin."

"Yes," Charles responded. "I was quite keen to take it up but when I started devilling under Adam, I was so busy I didn't have the time."

"How is that going?" asked Malcolm.

"Very well thank you," replied Charles. "I'm really enjoying it."

"You should become a member of the Speculative Society at Old College. It's a good place to practise your debating skills," remarked William.

"Yes," agreed Charles. "Adam had mentioned the Society."

"They're always looking for debating subjects," said Malcolm.

"Ladies and gentlemen," announced Lord Hugh. "I'd like to have a word with Mr McLeod. Would you excuse us while we go to the study for a glass of port?"

"Yes of course father," replied Amelia.

When the two gentlemen had retired Charles leant forward, clasped his hands and in a serious tone said, "Adam asked me to come up with a suggestion and I think the Society should have a debate about the current situation. Something along the lines of …Is the Government justified in introducing draconian measures which curtail freedom of speech vs should not the populace have a right to freedom of expression in a democracy?"

Malcolm puffed. "That *is* a serious subject."

"Well," responded Charles. "I think it is apt. We should be debating current issues rather than centuries old events such as Charles 1 execution. We're lawyers – at least I'm training to be one – and we should be debating and discussing remedies for the current political unrest."

Amelia emphatically piped up, "I think that is a very good idea."

"Well, I don't think it is an apt discussion for a debate," remarked William, "because ultimately there is nothing to debate. The status quo is as it is – immovable. It's a futile gesture on the populace's part to even contemplate change."

"How can you be so adamant?" enquired Amelia.

"Yes," Charles agreed. "How can you be so adamant considering there are hundreds of thousands asking the government to pledge change?"

William pointedly said, "It won't make any difference. I don't see the point in revolt. Apart from the fact it's dangerous stirring up uneducated minds to push for change."

"But don't you think it healthy to at least have a debate about it?" asked Amelia.

"I don't see the point," reiterated William. "And I don't think that subject would be a welcome choice for a newcomer to suggest to the Society."

"Why ever not?" Charles asked.

"Because, apart from agent provocateurs such as Muir, almost all lawyers are in support of the Government, so there wouldn't be anyone to argue the other side."

"I would like to," Charles enthusiastically told him.

"Well of course Gillies respects Muir, so I suppose you're being encouraged to take his point of view."

"Not at all," Charles adamantly responded. "I'm coming up with my own opinion. I don't want to be influenced by other views. I'm personally analysing the pros and cons of what is happening and I do think it important lawyers consider both sides of the argument."

"Yes. If there was an argument," retorted William.

"But surely," said Amelia, "it is important for other opinions to be taken into consideration, not just the Government's."

"If the opinions of the radicals were reasonable, then there could be a discussion about it," said William. "But they're not. They're creating an atmosphere of sedition."

"That's a strong word William," remarked Amelia. "I think their demands for good representation are perfectly reasonable and - rational."

"Gosh Amelia," said William, "you're certainly becoming opinionated."

Amelia adjusted her posture, straightened her back and retorted "I've been reading the papers on a regular basis for months and I sympathise with their arguments."

"There you go William," remarked Malcolm. "That's put you in your place!"

William smiled at Amelia and said, "I beg to differ." He then looked at Charles and said, "Good luck with coming up with a topic for debate. But not that one. And I do advise, if you happen to sympathise with the rebellers, that you keep your opinions to yourself if you want to advance in your career."

"Good gracious," remarked Amelia, "are you saying Charles' future career is in jeopardy if he doesn't tow the Government line?"

"I think that would be an accurate comment Amelia," said William.

She was flabbergasted, "Well. So much for living in a democracy."

"Amelia," said William, adopting a benign tone. "This so called political crisis, will soon be over. You shouldn't get so het up about it. These things will be resolved. Give it time. You shouldn't get worked up about political affairs. They're like shifting sands in a storm, constantly changing, you never know how the terrain will look after it."

"Perhaps," she conceded.

"You're a marvellous pianist," he told her. "You should attach passion to that, rather than the news."

"But I love absorbing information. As Malcolm knows, my education didn't involve anything other than the arts, or how to comport myself. Now, I'm enjoying having a mind."

"You'll always have a mind Amelia," said William. "I shouldn't doubt that. But perhaps contemplate holding less radical values."

Benjamin entered the room to announce the sedan chairs had arrived.

William was the first to stand up and, smiling, said to Amelia, "Despite our differences, I thoroughly enjoyed the evening. Thank you so much to both you and Miss Charlotte."

"It was a pleasure," Amelia responded.

"Yes," said Charles, now at the door, "it was a pleasure to meet you all again and William, no doubt we'll be seeing one another around Parliament House. And you too Malcolm."

"Indeed we will," replied Malcolm. "Good luck."

"Goodnight to you all," said William giving a little bow as he was leaving. "See you on Monday Malcolm."

"Yes," replied Malcolm.

Charlotte, flute in hand, kissed Amelia on the cheek and said, "See you soon. Let's do it again."

"I'd love to," replied her friend.

Malcolm and Amelia sat in silence for a brief moment until their father came in. "Thank you my dearest for a delightful recital. We must do it again. And we must invite William soon for supper, don't you think Amelia?"

"Yes father. That would be very nice."

"Well my dears. I'm going to retire. Goodnight to you both."

VII

John spent days after the meeting agonising as to what he should do. He would have liked to have ignored the issue of whether or not he should join a society but knew it was impossible for him to do so. At work, he had to typeset the latest news. Walking anywhere in the city he was confronted with pamphlets and handbills pinned to every public notice board, and then of course ripped down and flung onto the ground. These days, every street in the city was littered with these discarded notices.

He had, he knew, to contemplate the pros and cons. Would it be wise to jeopardise his job, his livelihood if he was to join? Would there be any way he could keep it secret from his work colleagues? Up to now, John had been monosyllabic in his response any time James had made an occasional comment, and didn't engage. And that was a good thing because he wouldn't be avoiding a subject that was never discussed. But the MacFadyen family? Mr MacFadyen had made it perfectly clear that no-one should get involved, so if he did, that would mean he couldn't discuss it with them.

Then there were the risks. He could lose his job, become unemployed and God help him, become a destitute beggar. No - his practical mind told him - he would not. He could leave the city and get work on the land. But …he could get arrested and have to languish in prison for goodness knows how long. What a conundrum! No sooner had he made a decision than his mind would start revolving all over again. The inner turmoil was exhausting. The dilemma felt like cutting his soul in half. Practically, he said to himself he would be a fool to get involved but emotionally he felt drawn to the cause. But at the end of the day, if his conscience was berating him for not getting involved, so be it.

He continued to turn things over in his mind. If he wasn't meeting Peter after work, instead of seeking sanctuary in Creech's bookshop as he would normally do, he paced the streets of the city in an endeavour to clear his mind. He couldn't ignore the discarded pamphlets everywhere he walked but, still, the pacing did help to calm the turbulence so that by the time he returned to his lodgings he felt more relaxed. Mrs MacFadyen was however concerned for him. She had noticed he had lost his appetite and that he looked permanently exhausted. He reassured her that he was fine, but when he retired to his bed he was so fraught trying to come to a decision that he spent most of the night tossing and turning.

And walking to work in the morning he would say to himself - why should he even be contemplating a decision? Surely, his best course of action, and the most sensible course of action, would be to let life continue as it was

– with no reverberations. That would be the easy route, but somehow he had become stirred emotionally and it was seemingly impossible for him to ignore that, however much as he wanted to. But what would the advantages be of joining? Would there be any benefit? Would it beneficial for him to be isolated from his colleagues and the family? Of course it wouldn't. It would damage his relations with them. But, he mused, he had not told them about being at the riot. He had managed to keep that to himself and Peter had never mentioned it since, so presumably he had forgotten about it. But, having deliberated at length, he could not erase from his mind the fact that he agreed with the demands. It seemed only right and proper to have fair representation and why shouldn't he participate in the momentum attached to the cause.

Should he? Shouldn't he? The arguments revolved around in his mind day in, day out until finally, after leaving work one evening, he made a decision. No longer would he take the stance of a disinterested, non- confrontational outsider, he would embrace the naked injustices, join a society and visit Alec.

As he started down the High Street, he felt his gait had altered. Before making the decision he had walked with bent shoulders of a man overburdened by a dilemma but now his gait reflected the confidence he felt having come to a decision. Walking purposefully, he ignored the beckoning of ladies of the night emerging from dark corners and continued on. Robertson's Close was deserted when he arrived but much noise was coming from the tall tenement block where large families were crammed into one room, often sleeping together on a bed of straw. He could hear babies crying, children squabbling, adults shouting and laughter and when he pushed the main door open, the noise in the tiny entrance was amplified. Alec's door was directly in front of him, and now full of self-assurance he unabashedly knocked on his door. After several minutes, he heard the lock being turned and Alec's wary face emerged. His expression altered immediately on recognising John and, with a welcoming smile, he quickly ushered him into the room locking the door behind him, "It keeps us private. Guid tae see you. I wasnae sure if you'd come."

"Weel. I thought I'd visit tae see whit ye're daein'."

"Jist the usual. Getting' on wi' typesetting a novel."

"Anythin' else?"

Alec looked puzzled "Whit dae ye mean?"

"Weel. I thought, as ye were at the meetin' ye might be printing pamphlets."

Indignant, Alec retorted, "Not I."

"Weel," replied John in a pensive tone, "I've decided tae join the movement."

Alec, adopting a cagey stance asked, "Fur whit reason?"

Without hesitation John replied, "Ma conscience." He paused. "Look," he said, raising his voice, "wud I risk ma job if I wasnae sincere?"

"That's true," Alec soberly responded. "Bit keep yer voice doon. I hae tae be careful. Spies are aboot an' I dinnae git visitors."

"I can assure ye," John told him, lowering his voice, "I am not a spy."

Alec's mood lightened. "I'll hae tae tak yer word fur it." Then he chortled, "I ken where ye work."

"Aye," said John smiling, "ye dae." and they shook hands heartily. Alec then picked up a knife at a nearby table and walked purposefully towards the right hand side of the printing press. He stopped at a specific point and began rocking his feet on a floorboard. Satisfied he was at the right location, he stepped aside, got down on his knees and put the knife in between the grooves in the chosen floorboard. He lifted the wood up, leant forward, put his arm in the hole and retrieved a book. He stood up and gleefully said to John, "Here's a' the quotations." He replaced the wood, strode over to John and handing him the book said, "Ye hae tae choose a short one. I've decided tae dae hand bills instead o' pamphlets. Even if it gets torn doon, it can still be read in the street on the yin side. So ...choose yin an' let's git tae work."

Alec had put small pieces of paper in certain pages of the book so they could readily be accessed, but John wanted to find the quote that had riled his father. Alec hadn't marked it but sifting through 'The Rights of Man' for several minutes, John found it. "This is it" he asserted.

"Which quote?"

"The one MacDairmid read oot aboot despotism."

"Richt," said Alec eagerly. "Let's git started. Bit," he paused, "we'll put Friends and Countrymen at the top. That'll attract attention, even if they're pulled doon."

"Guid idea."

"I'll git the roll o' paper set up on the press,"

John took the book over to the table where the cases for the wooden upper and lower types were compartmented in individual boxes contained in wooden frames. Nearby was a stand for manuscripts which he set the book on with the appropriate quote in view. He sat down. The upper type frame was positioned above the lower one and John deftly began picking up the appropriate type and, working from left to right, placed them upside down on the composing stick. He worked at a terrific speed and soon all the composing blocks were ready to be inked with the woollen ink ball.

"Well done," his friend congratulated him "Very impressive. You dinnae hae ony problem with spellin'."

"I love reading. Since I was a wee boy, if I didnae understand a word I'd work oot the phonetics and pronounce it the way it should sound. That's helps wi' spellin'."

"Weel, I've never seen anyone work wi' such a speed."

"I've been at it a few years," John modestly replied.

"Richt then," said Alec enthusiastically. "Let's git printin'." And taking the blocks over to the printing press, he made ready by placing the type onto the press type bed, locked up the form in position, turned the long handle and started the printing process. Alec's target was twenty hand bills and this was soon achieved. Once completed, he cut the paper into individual sheets and laid them aside.

"Weel done John," remarked Alec gazing at the hand bills. "They look grand."

"Aye. They've come up well," replied John, feeling very pleased with himself. "Bit – how are ye gaun tae put them up?"

"That's the difficult one. I hae tae be very careful." He went to the coat stand and picked up a large black coat. "This is a poacher's coat," he proudly told John. "I put them in the pocket wi' a wee hammer." He smiled.

"The best time is at ten, when they're hurling oot the contents o' their chamber pots. I dae ma best tae avoid the nightly douse."

"Guid for you,"

"Hae ye ever been stopped?"

"No yet," He smiled. "I enjoy daen it. Getting' the Magistrates a' worked up."

"Aye," said John smiling, "it wid be guid tae see their faces." Getting serious, he added, "I dinnae mind doin' the printing. Bit I'm nae gaun tae put them up."

"I dinnae expect ye tae. An' if I git caught, I'll say I did them a' myself."

"Thanks."

"Do ye hae time tae do anither?" Alec asked, adding, "Anither short one?"

"Why no."

Alec went to the stand, picked up Paine's book and started to quickly go through the pages. After a few minutes he said, "Aye. This yin will dae," and he recited the quotation: *"'Friends of Reform, be unanimous, active and steady, asserting and constitutionally establishing the rights of man, and be not weary of well-doing for by wisdom, prudence and courage, in due time ye shall reap if he faint not.'"*

"That's guid," remarked John. "Richt. I'll get started." Within a short time, he had completed the text, handed over the composing sticks to Alec who then set up the printing process all over again. After they had completed the run, and cut the paper into individual hand bills John announced, "I'd better git going. I'll come agin next week if ye like."

"Definitely. An' there's a meeting at Matler's tavern on Friday if ye want tae go."

"Aye that wud be guid. We could dae a couple mair efter the meeting."

"Guid idea," agreed Alec enthusiastically."

"It's at seven?"

"Aye. That's the time," Alec confirmed, walking behind him to the door. "Now, wheesht when ye leave and we'll see ye on Friday."

"Grand." They walked over to the door and Alec gently opened it. "See ye soon."

Although he was exhausted when he left Alec's, having had no proper sleep for nights he felt elated, happy in the thought he had a purpose to his life amongst like-minded people. He knew he would rest easy that night.

VIII

On the day he was meeting Amelia, John woke when the Tron Kirk struck seven and entered the kitchen quietly so as not to disturb Mrs MacFadyen. He wanted to have a bit of a wash and had collected a large bucket of water the night before from the well nearby. No one would remark on it as he frequently helped with the household chores, carrying buckets of water from the well and bringing logs up from the basement for the stove. He put the bucket on the floor of the kitchen and scooped a small amount out with a pan and stealthily set it on the stove. When it was warm, he wiped his face and hands, dried them with the end of his loose shirt, flattened down his hair, tucked his shirt in and left, wearing his Sunday best coat again. It was the final Tuesday afternoon he had off work and he wanted to make the most of the short time he and Amelia had together for goodness knows when they would meet again. James had commented on his perky state, and indeed, he was brimming over with excitement at seeing her again and telling her about his new adventures. When he arrived at Creech's, a few minutes early, the table at the window was already taken, but no matter, there was one free at the top corner that would be private enough. Foregoing coffee, he strode over and claimed it, picking up a chair on the way. As he sat down and eagerly awaited her arrival, the St Giles clock struck two.

Amelia too was quite excited about seeing John. Over breakfast, her father asked her what her plans were for the day. "I've got the art class with Charlotte this morning, and this afternoon I'm going to Creech's with Meg."

Her father smiled affectionately at her and remarked, "Your favourite haunt."

"Yes it is." She hesitated for a moment, deliberating whether she should tell him about her meeting with John but they had got on well so she did. "Meg and I are meeting John McCulloch at Creech's."

"Who?" asked Malcolm.

"You must remember John. He's the gamekeeper's son. He used to come to the house every summer for years."

"I think I met him a couple of times. I was always out and about round the estate."

"I remember him," said her father. "Nice chap. Is he still working at the *Caledonian Mercury*?"

"Yes. And enjoying it I think."

"How did you happen to meet up with him again?" asked Malcolm. "You don't exactly move in the same circles."

"I know" said Amelia brightly. "Father will appreciate this. We were both at Creech's book shop the other day and recognised one another, even after five years."

"Ah yes," her father said. "He was an avid reader I remember."

"It was you father who encouraged him…"

"And he who encouraged you to read my dear."

"It's true," she recalled.

"I certainly remember he was somewhat awestruck at the volume of books in the library."

"He felt very shy when he first met you," Amelia recounted. "And he was delighted when you lent him 'Gulliver's Travels'."

"I thoroughly approve of reading," said her father, "although I don't necessarily agree with Johnson's statement, 'a little knowledge is a dangerous thing'. Reading can enhance one's understanding of life and it is wonderful to immerse oneself in fantasy. Although now, the only earnest reading I do is of business reports. Still, I enjoyed it when I had the leisure time to do so. And thinking of work, I have to get on."

"Yes," replied Malcolm. "I have to get going soon as well. The courts are very busy at the moment…"

"Ah yes," his father wearily responded, heaving himself to his feet. "All those arrests." He sighed. "Hopefully it will all calm down and we can get back to normal..... whatever that may be. And Amelia, give John McCulloch my regards."

"Will do father," she called out as he was leaving the room. Malcolm and Amelia carried on eating their breakfast until Malcolm broke the silence by asking her, "What do you think of William Gilchrist?"

"He seems perfectly pleasant."

"He's a rising star at the bar, you know."

"I'm not surprised. He has that assured temperament."

"He's been asking a lot about you,"

Amelia chuckled. "I hope you've given him favourable comments."

"Of course I have. But," he paused. "he would make a good catch."

"Maybe," mused Amelia.

"And father approves of him," said Malcolm.

"Yes. I know."

"Anyhow, he's looking forward to seeing you at the ball."

"Yes. I'm looking forward to it as well. Charlotte was telling me we're going to be taught new country dances. That should be fun."

"But, getting back to William. Perhaps you should consider him as a suitor."

"Malcolm," she said in a slightly exasperated voice, "I'm hardly thinking about things like that. I'm just starting my life. I don't want to be burdened by having a suitor, or even having to contemplate marriage."

"There are plenty of women your age who are married. What's wrong with it?"

"Nothing at all," she quickly responded. "It's just not for me right now."

"Well. He's a decent chap. He's been of great help to me progressing my career at the bar. I couldn't have done without his help and advice. And as a favour sis, you could at least consider it. For me?"

"I suppose," she said in a resigned voice. "If you want me to, I will."

"Thanks sis." He stood up, pushed back his chair and said, "I have to be off. Countless prosecutions are lining up so it's going to be another busy day. See you later."

"Yes," she replied, wiping her mouth and putting her napkin on the table.

"I'll tell William you were asking after him shall I?"

"You can if you want to. I'm not bothered if you do, or don't."

"I'll tell him." And with that he left the room.

Amelia looked at the clock on the mantelpiece and realised she had better get organised for the art class as the sedan would soon be arriving.

The morning passed pleasantly enough. Mr Walker had placed a selection of apples, with various hues, in an attractive beige enamelled tin bowl. It was a challenge to paint the variety of subtle colours and the group sat at their easels in silence, absorbed in concentration mixing the tones with the water colour paints. Amelia wasn't entirely focused on the task in hand as she was contemplating Malcolm's comments. When Charlotte commented on her pre-occupied state at the break, she dismissed it saying she had had a restless night. Her friend and the other ladies accepted the explanation. What she was thinking about though was that she didn't want to be burdened by having a suitor. She found William attractive but she didn't know what the expectations of love were and was quite sure she did not want to be pressured into making any decision simply because he was Malcolm's closest friend. She much preferred the freedom of choosing her own friends and was pleased John and she had rekindled their friendship. It was a pleasure being with someone who had known her in her youth and been part of her short history. Who knows what the future would hold but she was determined that when it came to making decisions about her life – certainly if it came down to marriage – that she would not be influenced by anyone, including her father, if it was not what she wanted. But why should she even bother to think about it? She was now more interested in keeping abreast of current affairs than organising tea parties for the ladies. That may be in the future, but certainly not now. And that was the attitude she had adopted when the carriage arrived to take her and Meg to Creech's bookshop.

When she arrived at Creech's, John's heart gave a little flutter. He thought she looked stunning, as did the other men in the room who gave her admiring glances as she glided past towards his table. "How nice to see you," she said smiling as she approached.

"Aye," he returned the smile, "it's good to see you too. Now, settle down, I've got lots of news." He leaned towards her once she was seated and said in a low voice, "I've joined the movement."

"Good gracious!" she blurted out.

"Keep your voice down," he urgently told her. "You have to be careful who's listening."

"What happened?"

"I have a conscience. I was reminded of your comment last time we met."

Surprised, she said, "You shouldn't take everything I say to heart. "

"I do," he responded, watching as Meg arrived with the coffees.

"How are you today Meg?"

"Very weel thank ye Sir."

"It's John," he reminded her in a friendly voice.

"Yes, John will do," said Amelia pleasantly. "Now Meg, if you don't mind, John and I would like to have a tête-à-tête. Would you mind amusing yourself by looking out the window at the passers-by?"

"Certainly m'am."

They huddled together and John, ignoring some disapproving looks in the room, started to recount, in detail, the story of what had happened. Completely absorbed in the narrative, she didn't interrupt until he concluded by asking if she had seen handbills in the High Street recently. "Good gracious," she exclaimed. Then lowered her voice, "They're not your doing are they?"

"I'm proud to say they are," he told her, smiling.

"Well," she responded, astonished by his tale "But you must be careful."

"Aye. I will be," he assured her.

"Malcolm and our friend William Gilchrist are prosecuting so many people on a daily basis…"

"It's sure to be resolved soon."

"William was saying the other evening – Father had organised a small soiree and he had been invited…"

"Do you still play the piano?"

"Oh yes. But," she chortled, "do you remember the fuss I would make about having to practise?"

"I do indeed," he smiled at her warmly. "You were like a spoilt child not being able to get their own way. You were ridiculous."

"I've changed," she demurely responded. "Anyway," she resumed, "William said politics are like shifting sand in a storm - you never know how the terrain will look when it abates. He also said it will soon be resolved."

"Hopefully in our favour."

Still huddled together, she said, "I think it's wonderful what you're doing. Father and I are all for the reform demands. But – do be careful. They're already arresting so many people. And besides, you could lose your job."

"Yes I know. I spent days agonising before I made the decision. But I feel calm, strangely enough. It's what I want to do. I went through all the ramifications of making this decision, but truly my conscience dictated the final decision. I didn't make it lightly."

"I can see that." She paused. "I would feel better if there weren't so many arrests being made."

"But as Alec said, there are too many people involved in the movement and they can't arrest them all. I feel fine about it."

"I hope you're right," she gravely responded.

"Now," he sat up, spoke at a normal volume, and asked, "What have you been doing, apart from entertaining people at the soiree?"

"Actually," she earnestly replied. "I had to practise rather a lot for that. My friend Charlotte plays the flute and we were learning a Mozart duet." She twitched a little and said, "It probably sounds rather frivolous to you, but I loved doing it."

"Of course it doesn't found frivolous. You don't have to be consumed by daily events all the time. It's very important to stop the mind revolving and engage in something that gives you pleasure."

"What do you do to relax?"

"I read when I can. I'm halfway through Pilgrims Progress. Have you read it?"

"No. Not yet. But if you recommend it, I will." She paused a moment. "I like painting. I go to an art class on a Tuesday and Thursday…"

"You were there this morning?" he asked.

"Yes, with my friend Charlotte. Mr Walker is good teacher; he always creates an inspiring still life for us to paint."

"It's good to have a friend. Peter is mine. He's a caddie. Nice lad." The clock at St Giles struck three quarters of the hour. "Anyway, I'd better get back to work."

"Will you be here next week?"

"No. That's the end of time off during the day."

"Why don't we meet one evening at the Circulating Library? It'll be in Parliament Close next Tuesday."

"I'm not a subscriber."

"That's not a problem. You can just join up. It's only twelve shillings for half a year, or a guinea for a year.

They've got a very good range of novels, poetry, reviews and magazines."

"That sounds good." He did a hasty calculation as to whether he could afford the half year cost. He had a small amount of money saved, so decided he could. "I finish work usually about seven. Would that be a good time for you?"

"Yes. That would be convenient."

"If I do have to work late, I could get Peter to drop off a note at your house. He's often around that part of town. But, hopefully it'll be fine."

He stood up to leave. "Good day Amelia. I look forward to seeing you then. Goodbye Meg," he said, interrupting her reverie.

"Guid bye sir. Oh," she smiled. "I mean John."

He nodded goodbye to them both and hurriedly left. Although he was thrilled they were going to be meeting again soon, he knew he would have to make an effort to curb the feelings he was now having for Amelia. The mention of the soiree grounded him. He could never offer her that type of life. Just treat her as a friend, he told himself. Nothing more. Nothing less.

IX

William was certainly not thinking of affairs of the heart as he awaited Jock's arrival at his lodgings. They had been having regular meetings for several weeks on Monday evenings and he was proving to be a diligent spy, adept at keeping a low profile in the meetings but capable of blending in with members and eliciting valuable information from them. But they'd had to put it forward to the Tuesday because the day before had been Thanksgiving Day, a public holiday where everything was closed, no meetings were allowed, but everyone was required to attend an annual special service at church in which the Ministers read out the text of the Observance of the 5th November Act, a date the country commemorated the failed attempt by Guy Fawkes on King James 1 life. When it had happened, people in London had lit bonfires in thanksgiving that the King had survived the attempt on his life and months later Parliament introduced the Act. Although he had not been at court, but of course had attended a service, it was not necessarily a quiet day for him immersed as he was in the mound of charges he would be prosecuting that week.

The movement was gathering momentum, pamphlets and handbills with Paine's quotations were to be seen everywhere in the city. William thought it was getting out of hand. More measures had to be taken. The militia would have to be increased and perhaps more Town Guards appointed. Everything had to be done to ensure the situation did not erupt as it had done in France. He had recently read that King Louis was not only confined to his room in the Temple, but his windows had been blackened to ensure he couldn't pass any messages to anyone, and he was deprived of even pen and paper. His only contact was with his jailers. It was unthinkable that that could happen to King George. Order therefore had to be maintained at all costs. The rebellers could not have their demands met.

Jock arrived promptly at seven. William ushered him into his study and, even before offering him a seat, asked in a forthright manner, "So what's the latest?"

"I think you'll be interested in this. I ken a coachman who does the Glasgow route frae the White Hart. I saw him on Friday and he telt me Thomas Muir wis gaun tae be holdin' a meeting in Kirkintilloch on Saturday tae tak aboot reform."

"Well," William said, taking a deep breath, "stirring people up with his inflammatory words will not be doing his career any favours. Silly man." He paused then asked, "Anything else?"

"Aye," Jock eagerly responded, and retrieved a notebook from an inside pocket of his jacket. Turning a few pages, he eventually found what he was looking for. "I've been tae a couple o' meetings – yin at Laurie's Rooms in the Lawnmarket an' the ither at Matler's. I noticed anither man hae started tae attend so I kept an eye on him. He seemed tae be getting paly wi' a guy called Alec. I think he's a printer."

"Check him out," William told him. "It can't be that difficult to find out where he works. There are only about sixteen printing establishments in the city. See if you can surreptitiously visit them. And," he added. "Find out what the other man's name is."

"I think it's John."

William, in a pointed tone, said, "I want you to follow them when you can and report back."

"They left the meeting at Matler's th'gither. I wis gaun tae follow them bit I wis already speakin' tae someone an' they wid hae thought it odd if I'd rushed aff."

"Well, keep a check on them if you see them again. We have to find out where these new handbills are being printed." Furious, he added, "It's disgraceful what they're doing."

"Aye. I ken."

"So there are a few new members?"

"Aye."

"Any idea where they're coming from?"

"Ma freend the coachdriver talks tae ither drivers when he gaes tae Glasgow. And he wis saying they're joining frae a' the trades - weavers, cobblers, brewers, bakers. Haud on…there's mair – oh aye …tanners and butchers."

"What a riff raff," William disdainfully remarked. "Anything else?"

"Hae ye heard o' a Captain Johnston?"

"Indeed I have. Why, what's he been doing?"

"He's going tae be setting up a newspaper, the *Edinburgh Gazetteer.*"

Curious William asked, "What does he intend to print in it?"

"Seditious material, so I hear."

"Well, we'll have to get the reporters on the Edinburgh Herald to counter any of his comments." He paused. "When is the first paper to be published?"

"In ten days' time, on the sixteenth. It's tae be a weekly."

"It'll be interesting to read what scandal they're going to be publishing. Anyway Jock, you're doing a good job. Continue to keep your ear to the ground, and we'll stop these rebellers yet."

"Indeed we will sir."

"And this is for your good services so far," William said, handing him two guineas.

"Thank ye sir! Glad tae be appreciated."

Although pleased with the money William had given him, when Jock left he started to think about William's offensive riff raff remark. He was irked by it. These were hard working people he was commenting on. He may not agree with their political views, but they shouldn't be spoken of in this disrespectful way by people like William. He was still thinking about it when he crossed over to St Giles but didn't have time to deliberate further because, when he glanced into Parliament Close, he was struck by the sight of a young couple standing underneath a street lamp beside the Circulating Library. Talking amiably, they were quite a contrast. She was obviously a lady, and looked elegant in her hooded, full length cerise pelisse. Even in the dim light of the close he could see a cerise pattern embroidered on her black, small heeled pointed leather boots. He, on the other hand, was obviously not a gentlemen wearing as he was thick leather boots, working man's breeches, a common man's plaid and clasping a working man's cap in his hands. He looked again at the man and immediately recognised him as the 'John' who had left the meeting with Alec. But who was the young lady? Nearby was a sedan with two chairmen waiting for someone. Maybe they were taking her home? Maybe he could find out who she was? As he approached the chairmen of the sedan, a group of men were noisily passing so he quickly took the opportunity of going up to one of them and surreptitiously asking, "Are ye waiting fur the lady ower there?" he glanced in the lady's direction.

"Aye," replied the man.

"A gentleman friend o' mine wud like her address."

"Oh," replied the man. "I'm no so sure aboot that."

Jock put his hand in his pocket, retrieved some coins and furtively handed the man two shillings. "Maybe this will help ye change yer mind." The man was delighted at this generous amount and readily agreed to do as he was asked.

"Meet me at the White Horse in an hour."

"Aye. I will," the man replied as Jock walked away. Instead of going directly to the White Horse though he decided to wait in the shadows in the High Street, near the Parliament Close entrance, to see if he could follow the man.

Eventually, the sedan chair emerged transported by the chairmen, one on either end, and accompanied by a link boy carrying a lantern. Jock slunk into the shadows as it passed by, followed by the man who proceeded to walk down the High Street. Quite a few people were about so it was possible for Jock to stalk him unobserved. Optimistic the man would lead him to a printer's office, he was disappointed when he turned into a close opposite Blackfriars Street. Several paces behind, Jock stealthily followed him into the dark close listening to the footsteps mounting the stairs, right to the top floor, when he heard a door being opened and a female voice calling out, "Is that ye John?" "Aye Mrs MacFadyen," the man replied and the door was closed. Satisfied he now knew where this John lived, he walked back down the stairs resolved to return early in the morning to wait in another close entrance until John emerged. Then he would follow him to his work place.

X

William, as usual, had a busy week at court with Malcolm proving to be skilful at cross examining people in the dock. And socially, it was a delightful week. William and Malcolm were good friends and Malcolm was aware of William's intention to become Amelia's suitor so he had asked him to visit the house for a few glasses of claret. Amelia was there with Charlotte and they spent an extremely pleasant time together discussing future soirees and the forthcoming Caledonian Hunt Ball at the Assembly Rooms. Later in the week he took Malcolm to his first cockfight in a pit in Leith. A popular sport, it was held in the ground floor of a warehouse. Packed with men of all classes, the noise was deafening with bookies shouting out the odds on particular roosters, who had all been specifically trained to be aggressive. The birds were caged and when the starting bell was rung they were taken out of their cages and placed beak to beak in the small ring, both wearing long, dagger-like attachments with the sole purpose of inflicting great pain, or death on their opponent. Malcolm found it quite distasteful, describing it as a gruesome sport, and they didn't stay till the fatal end.

On the Thursday they went to the Pantheon Society. William had become a member and Malcolm was able to join him as his guest. A debating society, the topic that week was 'Whether is the Drunken Husband or Scolding wife more destructive of Domestic Happiness?' Every man in the room was familiar with the saying 'every gentleman a drunkard and every drunkard a gentleman.' Gentlemen being drunk was de rigeur in the upper eche-lons of society but, it was argued, it would depend on the attitude of the drunken husband towards his wife. If the husband exhibited cruelty towards the lady, be it physical or emotional, that would certainly not bode well to any state of domestic happiness. However, if the husband had not provoked the wife when drunk then her scolding could be termed as being irrational and unreasonable. Certainly, unreasonable scolding could, without a doubt, affect domestic happiness. But if the drunken husband displayed irrational behaviour towards his wife then that of course would profoundly affect domestic happiness. It was a lively debate concluding with the comment it would all depend on the attitude, temperament and actions of the individuals involved as to whether they could be deemed to be destructive to domestic happiness.

Then on the Friday evening he went to a recital at St Cecilia's Hall. He did see Amelia and although he tried to attract her attention, she was engaged in conversation with others and so he didn't have a chance to speak. However, another glimpse of her could be had on the Sunday at Hugh Blair's sermon at the High Kirk. He always chose a specific topic for his sermons and that week it was the slave trade. William had noticed the cameo Amelia was wearing but chose not to comment on it as he personally thought the trade should not be abolished because of the revenue it brought to the country, but he knew Amelia was keen to promote awareness of abolition and perhaps he might alter his mind to gain her favour. All in all, he thought he had had a delightful week and had Jock's news on Monday evening to look forward to.

Jock meanwhile had turned up expecting to see John leaving Mrs McFadyen's at seven thirty, the morning after seeing him arrive there. However, when he heard the Tron kirk strike eight there was still no sign of him. Frozen to the bone after standing all that time in a draughty open close, he decided to leave and come another morning. He didn't consider John to be of importance to the movement so he wasn't attaching any urgency about stalking him. There was another meeting at Matler's which he noted John attended and when the meeting finished he saw John and Alec leaving together. He followed them out into the street. They had a brief talk outside but soon parted company going in opposite directions. Jock was in a dilemma. Which man to follow? He chose John, but to his disappointment, he returned to his lodgings.

Although Jock visited a few taverns over the following evenings in the hope of eliciting information from conversations, it wasn't until the Friday he had some success. He had decided to go to the fish market first thing that morning. Dawn had broken as he was walking down the High Street and, despite the smoky haze he was able to clearly discern John approaching Old Fishmarket Close and turning into it. Jock burst into a run and reached the entrance to the close just as John was opening a door half way down on the left hand side. Jock didn't linger, but he would make a point of asking a caddy what businesses were conducted in the close.

Always on the prowl for new information he went to the White Hart Inn that evening where he met up with his coachman friend who told him some very interesting news. Through his coachmen contacts in Glasgow he had heard that Thomas Muir was distributing and circulating Paine's book in Glasgow, Kirkintiloch, Lennoxtoun and Miltoun. And he was letting it be known he was available at any time to talk about the contents in the book at any meeting.

On Monday morning, Jock met up with a caddy, asked about the premises in Old Fishmarket Close and was told it was the printing office of the *Caledonian Mercury* newspaper. Jock asked the caddy if he knew of a person called John who worked there. The caddy did and Jock was told he was a typesetter for the paper. Now that was interesting news to tell William that evening.

John too had had a busy week. He had started to leave early most mornings to go to Alec's to work on more hand bills before going to do his shift at the paper. It meant he was able to see his friend Peter in an evening and they met up at the Beehive Inn where there were booths and they could have a private conversation. He had decided to tell Peter about the recent events in his life and didn't want to be overheard. He was a good friend so he wanted to share the news with him. They settled down with their pints of ale in an empty booth at the back of the inn.

"Whaur hae ye been?" Peter asked. "I huvnae seen ye in ages."

"I've been busy."

"Obviously," his friend retorted. "Bit whit hae ye been doin?"

They were sitting opposite one another and John leant forward towards his friend and in a low voice told him, "I've joined the movement."

Taken aback Peter responded, "Ye'r mad. Whit on earth persuaded ye tae dae that?"

Earnestly John replied, "As I said to Amelia. It's ma conscience."

"Amelia?" his friend quizzed. "Who's Amelia. Ye've no mentioned her name afore."

"I'll tell ye in a minute. First of all, I'm glad I've done it." He paused as Peter leant towards him digesting the news. "It wasnae an easy decision. I deliberated fur days, bit I'm glad I've made it."

"Bit it's dangerous," his friend replied in a concerned tone.

"Och no. As Alec said …"

"Whae's Alec?"

"Hud on a meenit," John smiled. "It'll all be revealed. I bumped into that man we'd spoken tae at Fortune's. Dae ye mind o' him?"

"Aye. The man that seen ye at the riot?"

"Aye. That's him. Weel, it wis an evening ye wurnae able to meet up and I hud nothing else tae dae so he asked me tae come tae the meeting and I went along. Then efter, in the pub, I git talkin' wi' a printer called Alec. And the fact o' th' maiter is…" he stopped, not sure whether to tell his friend or not in case it could affect their friendship.

"The fact o' th' maiter is whit?" Peter asked in an irritated voice.

"I dinnae ken if I shuid tell ye…"

"Go on," persuaded Peter. "We're friends. We shuid be able tae tell yin anither al' oor thoughts."

"Richt then. I will. I'm typesetting the hand bills that are being put up in the High Street."

Horrified, Peter said emphatically, "That's awfy foolish! "

"I'm no worried aboot it. I'm just glad I'm able tae help oot."

"I shouldn't be sae nonchalant aboot it," his friend stated. "I wasn't gaun tae tell ye cos I didn't think it important at the time, bit a caddy mate telt me there wis a man asking whit ye did at the paper. Ye maun mind oot," he warned his friend.

"It'll be fine," John reassured him.

"Well, dinnae git tae cocky," his friend told him. "Mind yer back. Dae the MacFadyen's ken?"

"No. I'm nae telling them anything. They wouldn't approve anyway."

"Jist be very careful," Peter warned him. "I dinnae want tae hear ye've been arrestit."

"Och," replied John, unconcerned. "I'm sure that'll no happen. As Alec said, there are ower mony folk involved fur them a' tae git arrested."

"Maybe."

John leant back in his chair and said, "An' there's something else. It's a bit o' a problem."

"Anither yin?" his friend smiled at him.

"Aye. Anither yin. I've met up again with ma childhood friend Amelia. My faither's the gamekeeper on her faither's estate and we used to play th'gither every summer fur years. I bumped into her at Creech's, we started chatting and we're seeing yin anither every week noo."

Bemused his friend asked, "Whit's the problem wi that?"

"Nithin'. Nithin' at all ..... except I think I'm falling fur her an' nithin' will come o't."

"How no?"

"She's a lady," John replied in a resigned voice. "We come frae different backgrounds. I coudnae expect her tae marry me when I've sae little tae offer in terms o' comfort. Onyway, it'll no happen so there's nae point in even thinking aboot it. But," he said, perking up. "I love being in her company. An' she's bonny. The most beautiful woman ye coud ever imagine."

"Oh dear. Ye've got it badly," said his friend empathising with his plight.

"Weel," John calmly replied "I'm gaun tae dae a' I can tae curb ma emotions an' jist enjoy her company. Nothing else."

"That's a' ye can dae," his friend agreed.

"That minds me. We're supposed tae be meetin' next Tuesday but I've been asked tae work late that evening. Could you drop a note tae her hoose? I'll suggest another time."

"Whaur does she live?"

"Queen Street. Number eighty-one."

"Aye. I'll dae that."

"Thank ye. An' could ye get her reply?"

"Nae problem," his friend replied. "Wud ye like anither ale?"

"Na. I'm awfy tired. I'm getting up early tae go tae Alec's sae by mid-evening I jist want tae get tae ma bed. Are ye staying?"

"Aye. I'll see if I can git some business here."

John stood up. "See ye in the next couple of days. Same place? Same time?"

"That'll do fine," Peter agreed. "Til then, tak care ma freend."

John did heed his friend's advice and started to make a point of checking to see if he was being followed. And although he was kept busy working on the illicit hand bills and his long shifts, Amelia constantly pervaded his thoughts, much to his consternation.

And much to Amelia's consternation, she was constantly thinking of John. Of course she attempted to dismiss it because it couldn't come to anything. Their lives were completely different. But what she liked about John was his lack of pomposity. She was feeling the constraints of her upbringing quite profoundly now, and she yearned to return and continue to be her own free, enquiring spirit. She knew John would welcome that. And she felt relaxed in his company.

However, she too immersed herself in other things in an endeavour to occupy her mind elsewhere. She and Charlotte were going to give another soiree. A Mozart duet again but this one required an inordinate amount of practice. She and Meg also visited Creech's a few times. She knew John wouldn't be there but she enjoyed the atmosphere of the coffee room, although she made a point of ignoring the appreciative glances from some of the men.

At the art class she was encouraging conversations on the slave trade and comments on Mary Wollstonecraft's book, even when the group were painting. This was much to Mr Walker's chagrin as he asked, in a slightly exasperated tone, if she could please refrain from making inconsequential comments when the ladies were attempting to focus on their artworks. But she persisted, albeit gently, in expounding her thoughts.

She also started dancing classes with Charlotte at Mr Clark's dancing school. He looked like a theatrical character with his powdered wig and pigtail with curls at his ears. He had ruffles at his breast and wrist and wore black silk breeches, white silk stockings and ankle boots with large silver buckles. The classes took place in the Assembly Rooms in George Street where they were taught minuets, reels and country dances. It was a perfect distraction and thoroughly enjoyable.

And William had certainly made his presence felt that week. But, she realised, she was pre-occupied elsewhere, and was reminded of that when Meg handed her a note from John on the Friday. Her heart gave a flutter as she opened it. 'Could we meet on the Monday evening at the Circulating Library at seven? I have work commitments on the Tuesday.' 'Yes of course I can, and I so look forward to seeing you again' she wrote in her florid style and signed it 'Amelia.' John too reacted when he got her reply. His heart gave a little lurch when he read the note and thought what beautiful handwriting she had.

XI

On Monday, before going to William's lodgings, Jock decided to go to Parliament House to check if there was a note from William in his pigeonhole, postponing the meeting as had once happened. No note was there so he made his way to the lodgings. As he stepped out of the main door into Parliament Close he looked to where the Circulating Library was and saw John again with the lady. To his astonishment, he witnessed him take the lady's gloved hand in his, and kiss it. Well, that was another piece of news to tell William as he hurried to the lodgings.

"So Jock. What's the latest?" asked William when he arrived.

"Muir's been causing trouble I hear," responded Jock. "He's distributing an' circulatin' Paine's book in a few cities an' not only attending meetings but speaking at length aboot Paine and his quotes."

"Foolish man," stated William. "That could be termed as seditious behaviour. Good work Jock. Anything else?"

"Aye. I checked up on that man John. John McCulloch is his name. I've seen him at ither meetings an' fund oot he works as a typesetter at the *Caledonian Mercury*."

"Oh. That's interesting," William remarked.

"An' there's something else. When I left last week I saw him chatting tae a lady in Parliament Close."

"How do you know she was lady?"

"Her attire. I thocht I'd find out who she wis. There wis a sedan nearby so I asked yin o' the chairmen if they were taking her hame. They were, so I gave him a good tip an' asked him tae gie me her address. She lives in a hoose in Queen Street."

"Queen Street?" asked William, getting slightly agitated. "What number?"

"Eighty-one."

Trying to remain controlled William asked, "Are you absolutely sure?"

"Aye. I got the man tae tell me the address twice."

William could feel the blood draining from his face, but he certainly wasn't going to make a show of it in front of Jock. "And what did she look like, this lady?"

"She wis a bonny looking lady. She had long golden curls. Bit whit I wanted tae tell ye wis that I saw this John kissing her hand."

"Doing what?" William said, trying very hard to contain his fury.

"Aye. He wis kissing her gloved hand," Jock reiterated.

"How did she respond?" he asked, presuming she would have found it an impertinence.

"Actually, she didnae seem tae worried aboot it."

Taking an unobtrusive deep breath William sternly told Jock, "Follow that man - day and night. We have to find out if he's in league with the printer who's putting up handbills." He handed Jock two guineas. "If you need any more money for bribes, tips, whatever just get back to me," adding, "If there is any pressing news before our next meeting, leave a note at Parliament House."

"Aye. I will," replied Jock, accepting the money.

"You've done very well so far Jock. I'm pleased with your progress."

"Thank ye sir," said Jock, adding as he left. "Remember tae get a copy o' the *Edinburgh Gazetteer*. The first edition is oot this Friday."

"Well, the Edinburgh Herald is sponsored by the Government so their reporters will soon put Captain Johnston in his place."

"Aye. They will." Jock had noticed the pallor of William's face, but thought no more about it as he departed on his errand.

When the door closed, William sat at his desk which was strewn with briefs, notes from clients, meetings to be arranged, and listened to Jock's footsteps descending the spiral staircase onto the High Street. Opposite his window he saw grey clouds emerging above Parliament House. A storm was imminent and turbulence in the universe mirrored his dark mood.

Disregarding all the work to be dealt with on his desk, he focused entirely on the information he had just received from Jock. Flabbergasted, he stared into space and attempted to digest it. According to Jock, Amelia was carrying on an illicit affair with a typesetter. He pushed his chair back with a flourish, rose and began to pace the room. Any time he had to deliberate on a difficult case he would relentlessly pace the floor of Parliament Hall, and this news had indeed to be deliberated.

Forward and backward he strode. How could he have got it so wrong? He was convinced Amelia was starting to fall for him. He had seen a lot of her recently, making sure he was a frequent guest at their house. And how could she possibly have met this man? A typesetter of all people. He had no prospects. He would never be able to keep her in the style to which she was accustomed.

Jock must have got it wrong. But he saw them on two occasions and witnessed this man, kiss her hand. William was furious. This commoner had the audacity to kiss the hand of the woman he intended to marry.

He had planned to ask her to be his wife at the Caledonian Hunt Ball at the Assembly Rooms in just under two weeks' time. He had conjured up how he was going to do it. He was going to wait until midway through the ball, take her aside and ask for her hand in marriage. He was convinced she would respond with a 'yes'. And he knew there would be no problem with her father. They had a good rapport and he was, after all, one of Malcolm's oldest friends. But most importantly, he could not countenance failure, and he most assuredly was not going to be put off by a low-life youth.

Dusk had fallen. He approached the window, stopped and lit a large candle which was on the desk. When it was alight he caught a glimpse of his image reflected in the glass – rigid features, taut lips. Yes. He was determined to win her hand, nothing was going to stop him.

He began to pace again and contemplate a plan to get rid of this John McCulloch. Could he arrange to get him killed? Some low-life men died in drunken brawls in the city – one more would not make any difference. Jock had criminal contacts. But where could it be done – without any witnesses? That was the important issue. There would have to be no bystanders and according to Jock this man didn't spend hours in the taverns, so how could he be lured away? That would be difficult. And he couldn't ask Jock to do it, he would have to find another person and that would mean two people would be party to the crime. Then, they would have to be paid and they would know where the money was coming from.

He continued pacing, thought about the merits of the plan and came to the conclusion he could not risk getting involved in the deliberate death of another because if, by any chance, he was found out, that would be the end of his now flourishing legal career and he wasn't prepared for that to happen. He was young. Only twenty-three. He had his whole life before him and he had no intention of curtailing his career.

Night had descended. Shadows formed by the light of the candle as he paced back and forth and continued to contemplate. After a few minutes he was struck with an idea. He could get John arrested on a charge of seditious behaviour. But how could he manipulate evidence to secure his conviction? According to Jock, he was only a bystander at the Friends of the People meetings. The only evidence amassed so far was the fact he had been present at several of the meetings. That was it. Unlike Thomas Muir and William Skirving, who were becoming thorns in the Government's side, he wasn't a contributor. But seditious pamphlets and handbills were being printed. This John McCulloch worked as a typesetter and was becoming friendly with a printer. And even if it transpired he was not involved in illicit publications William was sure, with his legal training, he could concoct a case against him. He would though have to be discreet. No-one, apart from Jock, must know. And most particularly, Amelia must not know. If she was infatuated with this man, William must make absolutely sure that when he did get arrested, Amelia would have no indication whatsoever he had anything to do with it.

The stance he must take, he reasoned still pacing, was one of sympathy. That would ensure her hand. He returned to his desk chair, sat down, relieved he had found a perfect solution.

XII

John had had no plan for any intimacy on the evening Jock saw him kissing Amelia's hand. It had happened spontaneously. They were saying goodbye and all of a sudden he was kissing her gloved hand. Unbeknown to him, when he took Amelia's hand, she had felt a frisson of excitement course through her body but, aghast at his effrontery, he immediately put his hand in his pocket and in a flustered state lowered his head to hide his mortification.

"I'm so sorry Amelia," he mumbled. "Please forgive me for being so forward," and he cautiously lifted his head to look at her. Her blue pupils had completely transformed into the colour of pale grey and to his astonishment she was emanating love towards him.

"I don't mind John," she said, smiling affectionately at him. As they gazed momentarily at one another he felt such love towards her. Realising their circumstances, reality set in and he became even more flustered.

"Uh...Miss Amelia," he stammered. "I... I mean Amelia." They looked at one another in silence, each absorbing the revelation that had occurred and then averted their gaze from one another to camouflage the profundity of the event. Both choosing not to allude to what had just happened, Amelia found her voice first and asked, "Shall we meet again?"

"Aye," he responded, in a slightly dazed state.

Winter was approaching; it was going to soon be too cold to meet outside. Although Amelia didn't have to have a chaperone, unlike most other cities, it was difficult to create an excuse to go out during an evening even for a short while. Classes were only held during the day, and why – her father would ask – was she seeing Charlotte for such a short time of an evening? What possible excuse could she have to see John? Then she remembered the letter she had receiving that morning from the women's Abolition Society saying the Presbytery at the High Kirk had kindly offered the Society a room to hold meetings.

"I know what we can do," she excitedly told him. "The Women's Abolition Society are starting to hold meetings on a Monday evening at a room in the High Kirk. Father wouldn't mind in the slightest if I go to them and we could meet before."

"Aye," he animatedly responded. "There's John's coffee shop in South Bridge. We could meet there for a few minutes at six forty-five."

"And if you have to work, you could send me a note."

"Even if I don't have to cancel shall I send you a note anyway?"

"Yes," she enthusiastically replied. "I should love to hear from you." She shivered.

Concerned, he responded, "You must go. You're cold."

She smiled sweetly at him and said, "Yes I am."

"I'll write to you before Monday," he eagerly told her.

When she left him she felt so excited in the sedan journey back to her home. It was love. She knew it. But what to do? God only knows. Mrs MacPherson noticed her highly vivacious manner when she bade goodnight and commented on it, as did Meg when she was unfastening her stays in the bedchamber. Amelia however, brushed the enquiry off and hurriedly wished her good night as she wanted to spend the remaining time before she slept thinking of John.

John too was in a state after she left – a state of elation. He strode confidently down the High Street remembering the love she had emanated towards him. He felt joyous and decided he would eat his supper hastily and retire to write her a note. He felt so elated when he returned to his lodgings that Mrs MacFadyen, noticing his happy state had to remark, "Ye'v hud a guid day John. I huvnae seen ye in such guid spirits fur a lang while."

"Aye. It's been a guid day. A lang day though so I'll jist quickly eat my supper an' get awa tae ma bed."

"Weel. Glad tae see ye'r happy. Are we no Mr MacFadyen?"

"Indeed we are," her husband agreed.

John hurriedly ate his meal, wished them both a good night and retreated to his box room. Sitting on his bed, he picked up a small wooden box nearby, retrieved paper, quill and ink and began to write a restrained note to Amelia which he would give to Peter to deliver the next evening. "It was a pleasure to meet you again. I look forward to seeing you on Monday and hearing your news. John."

Over breakfast the following morning Malcolm commented, "William is keen to book a few dances with you at the ball."

"That's nice Amelia," remarked her father.

Slightly hesitantly she responded, "Yes. That would be nice."

"Very good," said Malcolm. "I'll tell him." He rose and stepped towards the door. "Another busy day at court," he said, "then William and I are going to an oyster bar and then a performance at the Marionville Theatre."

"Oh," remarked Lord Hugh. "What is the performance?"

"Sheridan's 'School for Scandal'. They're a good acting troupe."

"Well enjoy," his father responded. "Yet another social event."

"Indeed sir," replied Malcolm. And he left.

Amelia and her father ate in silence for a few minutes until he commented, "I like William. Don't you my dear?"

"Yes," she quickly replied, "He's very nice." She stopped because she couldn't think of anything else to say about him. He didn't feature in her thoughts at all but she couldn't tell anyone that.

"He's got good prospects you know. He would make an admirable husband …"

"Father," she interrupted. "I'm hardly thinking about marriage at the moment."

"But you will soon have to my dear."

"No I don't!" she indignantly retorted.

"Dearest," he said compassionately. "We have to think of your future. And William would make a fine husband."

"Do you think so father?"

"Why do you doubt it? He already feels a part of the family."

Abruptly Amelia said, "I don't want to talk about it."

"Well, hopefully my dear you might change your mind." And with that he rose from the table and called out, "See you at dinner," as he closed the door.

After her father had withdrawn she started to ruminate. Maybe the love she now felt for John was an infatuation. How could she possibly be in love with the gamekeeper's son? But ... she reasoned ...they were such good friends for so many years, of course she never thought of him as the gamekeeper's son. He was her friend. Her only friend in her solitary childhood. And it was wonderful to rekindle their friendship. And that was all it was, she assured herself until ... Meg handed her a note from John on the Friday and her heart gave a little flutter as she opened it. Thrilled to receive it, she asked Meg to wait a moment whilst she wrote a reply, curtailing her emotions. "It was a pleasure to meet with you too. And I also look forward to seeing you next week. Amelia." She handed it to Meg to give to Peter. When Meg left she let her mind wander, back to the incident when he laughed heartily at the prospect of her becoming a pliable wife. He knew her so well and it was such a pleasure spending time with someone where she didn't have to act like the perfect lady she was brought up to become. With John, she could be entirely her own self. But what could be done? It was such a conundrum.

That evening John and Peter met in a booth at the Beehive Inn and when they had sat down Peter said, "Ye look as though something guid hae happened tae ye. So, whit's the news?"

John could hardly contain himself and he blurted out, "She loves me."

Surprised Peter asked, "How dae ye ken?"

"Her eyes," John immediately replied. "We were saying goodbye – och – I won't go into it, but when she looked at me, I knew fur certain."

"So whit ur ye gaun tae dae?"

"I dinnae ken. It's a bit o' a shock."

Ever practical, Peter said, "Ye jist hae tae see how it goes."

John's enthusiasm dampened. "I cannae see how it can gang anywhere, bit mah heart is hers, an' there's no a thing I can dae aboot it."

"It's a sad state o' affairs," responded his friend in commiseration.

For several minutes they sat sipping their ale in silence. Then John said, "I dinnae want tae feel despondent yit. It's jist happened an' richt noo, I want tae savour this happiness. Who knows whit'll come o' it. Bit," he said brightening up, "cuod ye dae me anither favour? I'll pay ye."

"Whit is it?"

"Can ye tak' anither note tae her an' git the reply?"

"Course I will," he readily responded. "Ye'r a friend. I dinnae want ony money. If I can help ye oot, I will."

"Thank ye," he said to his friend and passed the note to him.

XIII

Jock had witnessed the note being passed. Standing in the busy inn sipping his ale he looked indistinguishable from most working men in the city. He had a beard, was wearing a cap and a rough dark plaid draped around his body and as he told William, he was able to follow John surreptitiously without him being aware of it.

"Very good," said William. "Now sit down," he promptly told him. "I want to hear the details."

Jock sat with his back straight, arms on his thighs and narrated his news. "Ivery morning this week I saw him coming up the High Street tae start his shift at eight."

"Did you wait beside his lodgings first thing?"

"I did fur the first couple o' days but he wis regular in his routine so I decided tae come frae ma place by the Lawnmarket an' watch him coming up the High Street. Well. The first night he went tae the Beehive Inn an' he met a caddy friend – I recognised he wis a caddy frae his lantern. I coudnae hear whit they were saying fur they were huddled th'gither in a booth at the back. Bit, I did see him pass a note tae his friend."

"And?" William impatiently asked.

"I wasn't sure who tae follow, but I made a decision."

"Which was what?"

"Tae follow the caddy and see where the note was gaun."

"Good idea. And where did he go?"

"He headed in the direction of Queen Street."

"Queen Street," William soberly repeated.

"Aye. There weren't that many people aroond at that time so I had tae be careful no tae be seen."

"And were you?"

"Na. I wis quite a few paces behind but when he stopped at eighty one I ran doon the steps of a dark basement nearby and waited."

"For long?" William asked, in a slightly irritated tone.

"Aye. Fur quite a wee while.

"And then?"

"I heard his footsteps as he passed by an' I saw him put a note in his pocket."

"There's something afoot," William said, sounding agitated. "And I want you to get to the bottom of it."

Jock sighed. "As far as I can see he has nithin' tae dae wi the printin'. Last week he saw his caddy friend twice. Oh – and they went tae the White Horse Inn and I saw John accept a note frae Peter. John looked mighty pleased tae git it. Then the following evening he went tae a meeting an' spent the ither nights at his lodgings." He paused. "I jist dinnae think he's involved."

"Well, I'm not sure about his innocence," William retorted. "I have a gut feeling about the man. I want you to monitor his movements from early morning. I'll pay you well. And you've only been following him for a week. Maybe he was taking time off? I feel sure he's involved and I want him caught. Is that clear?"

"Aye sir. I'll dae ma best an' see whit ma enquiries come up wi."

"Good man. Right Jock," said William rising. "You may go. And any urgent news, you know what to do."

"Aye. I'll let ye know. Oh," he said as he was leaving. "Did ye git a copy o' the *Gazetteer*?"

"Yes. I did. I thought their comment that the paper 'will arrest bad men in their career' rather amusing."

"Thon Burns is a subscriber. I hear he's gaun tae be publishing a poem in this week's edition."

"Well," William retorted. "There's gratitude for you. It was lawyers who first welcomed Burns to the city. He would be foolish to get on their wrong side."

"Aye. He'd better be careful."

"Yes. He should be," replied William. He retrieved coins from his pocket and handed Jock two guineas. "Good work Jock. There will be more next week and hopefully you'll have some evidence for me regarding that John."

"I'll dae ma best," said Jock and left.

Once Jock had gone William's attention focused entirely on how he could stop this liaison and he started his usual ponderous pacing. Maybe it was perfectly innocent? But....a working-class lad kissing the hand of a lady is not innocent, and according to Jock, she wasn't perturbed by it. So what did that mean? She couldn't possibly be in love with him. That was a preposterous thought. But why the note passing and this man's reaction at receiving a reply if it wasn't something more than friendship? He paced more. He couldn't mention it to Malcolm because of course he would wonder how William had found out about it in the first place. And William could hardly admit to having his spy check up on Amelia. That would not bode well for their friendship.

But it has to be stopped, William told himself as he continued pacing. He has to go. I'm not having my future plans disrupted by a typesetter of all people. But how on earth could she have met him? Is she writing a book and asked him to typeset it? Surely Malcolm would have known about that if she was. And social events? He goes to the same social events she attends and she certainly couldn't have met him at a recital. So, where did they meet? He pondered and paced some more. Ah. The Circulating Library. That's where they must have met. He stopped pacing. But they're still meeting so there had to be something in it. An infatuation with someone who is working class? It rarely happened. But it did occasionally. What was he to do? Dispensing with melancholia, he reminded himself he was in a powerful position - part of the Dundas team, he had a spy under his wing, had influential friends - of course he could get rid of this man. But it would be much easier if there was solid evidence. Yes, as a prosecutor, he could trump up charges against him, and at the moment the judges did not appear too bothered about solid evidence. The fact that he attended meetings was sufficient to get him arrested and imprisoned. But concrete evidence would be preferable, particularly if he was to assuage Amelia. He knew she wouldn't accept a guilty verdict on the strength of him just attending meetings. There had to be valid proof to convince her.

He looked at his cluttered desk and told himself he had to stop obsessing about the man. It would be dealt with in good time. Meanwhile he had other pressing commitments to deal with like stopping the insurrection. He was flabbergasted at the number of men becoming members of the Friends of the People societies. Hundreds of thousands throughout North and South Britain. It had to be stopped. But – his mind flitted back to John and he concluded - I want him to be guilty.

He paced a little more, deliberating as to what to do at the ball. He couldn't risk her saying 'no' to his marriage proposal, particularly as he had hinted to Malcolm he intended to ask for her hand at the ball, in the same fashion his father had asked his mother. He would have to be patient, until this John McCulloch was dealt with, then ask for her hand.

XIV

Amelia and Meg had great fun choosing the gown for the ball. They had opened up the mahogany clothes press with much excitement and viewed the array of pressed dresses and ball gowns. Meg was a perfect lady's maid as she intuitively knew the colours that would best enhance her mistress' appearance. She picked out the burgundy gown with the patterned linen skirt and Amelia readily agreed her choice. The gown had a fitted top, was slightly high-waisted and tucked at the waist, then ruched to allow the material to be pulled to the side to allow the patterned linen skirt to be displayed. The colour of the dress would highlight the ruby necklace Meg would interweave around Amelia's piled up curls. And to complete the outfit they took beige three-quarter satin length evening gloves from one of the drawers beneath the pressed compartment, and then chose the beige satin dancing slippers, secured by ankle ties and kept underneath the clothes press, to match the evening gloves.

Amelia felt so happy when she was preparing for the ball. She treasured the notes from John and was bursting to tell someone about her new found love. Would Meg gossip she wondered? Charlotte probably would. But she had to tell someone. Meg had made several comments about how happy she looked – and although she tried hard to disguise her joy at receiving notes from John, Meg could hardly have failed to noticed her animated state when she handed her notes from him. Yes, she decided, I will confide in her.

"Meg," she said, as her maid was adjusting the stays of the corset to emphasise her slender waist. "I have to tell you. Or maybe I shouldn't. No. I have to tell you." She paused. "I'm in love."

"I thought there wis something up m'am," replied Meg shielding her face from the mirror to disguise her excitement at the news. "Is it William?"

"Oh no!" Amelia exclaimed. Then hastily added, "It's a secret Meg. You must tell no one."

"It's John. Isn't it?"

"I know it's ridiculous. Of course nothing will come of it, but I have never felt such happiness." She shook her head. "I truly have tried, so hard, so often to rid myself of this passion but I can't." She paused. "There is nothing I can do about it."

"Just enjoy the moment m'am," said Meg philosophically.

"Yes," Amelia responded in a ponderous tone. "And there are few of those. But I treasure each one."

"Weel," Meg replied in a solicitous manner. "It will be oor secret m'am."

"Yes it will."

"Noo," said Meg firmly. "Let's get ye looking like the belle o' the ball."

Amelia and her father arrived at the Assembly Rooms in George Street by carriage. William was standing near the entrance anticipating her arrival and when she glided in on her father's arm he thought she looked stunning with her golden ringlets enhanced by the lace trimmed burgundy ball gown.

"Good evening Lord Hugh," then addressing Amelia, "If I may be so bold to say you look beautiful this evening."

"Thank you William," she sweetly replied.

"Yes," replied her father. "I quite agree with you William. Now. Isn't that a pleasant introduction to the ball my dear?"

"It is indeed father."

"Come this way. Malcolm and I have reserved a table," William said ushering them to the stairs that led to the ballroom on the first floor.

The Caledonian Hunt Ball was a highlight in the social calendar and provided much material for gossip at subsequent ladies' tea parties. Even as they approached the stairs, they could hear the throng of animated voices emanating from the ball room. And what a splendid sight greeted them when they entered the crowded room. A vast mirror at the far end, and two others on either side, captured the lights from the enormous cut-glass chandeliers and candlelit sconces surrounding the walls. Jewellery sparkled in the candlelight and fans were flapped, some to ensure heat from the candles would not melt their waxen faces, others to attract attention. Weaving their way amongst the crowded tables to join Malcolm, Amelia remarked, "Oh look. There's Robert Burns. He was at the recital last week. Did you see him William?"

"No I didn't. I was too busy looking out for you," he smiled. When they got to the table, as soon as he had arranged Amelia's chair he said, "Now Amelia, I would like to book a few dances with you this evening before any other handsome young man does. May I have the first and last?"

"Yes of course you can," she jovially responded, and made a little indent in her card for his chosen dances.

"And another?"

She smiled at him. "If you insist William, but I have to leave space for other partners."

"Yes of course you do," he smiled at her. "Now will you excuse me while I have a quick word with your father before the first dance begins?" And he went to sit beside Lord Hugh while Amelia struck up a conversation with her brother. Their table was close to where the musicians were already seated, and so the dancing was soon to begin.

"I was wondering William," Lord Hugh said, "if you would like to join us for Christmas at the estate this year?"

"I would be honoured Sir. Thank you for the invitation."

"Yes," continued Lord Hugh. "Robbie will have the venison all prepared for us. He does a very fine job."

"Robbie?" quizzed William.

"Oh. Robbie McCulloch. Our gamekeeper. Fine fellow."

At the mention of the surname, William's body went cold. Then his court skills came into play. "Does he have a family?" he asked Lord Hugh.

"Yes," he replied. "A son. John."

William attempted to disguise his interest in having a casual conversation about the man. "Does he work on the estate?" he asked.

"No," replied Lord Hugh. "Unfortunately there wasn't work available for him at the time."

"Does he have a job on another estate?"

"No. He's in the city. Working for the *Caledonian Mercury*."

William was rendered speechless by this revelation but, before he had the opportunity of deliberating on the news, a voice boomed out nearby, "Ladies and Gentlemen. Please take your partners for the first dance of this evening. A minuet."

Without excusing himself to Lord Hugh, he quickly rose from his chair and went over to Amelia. "My lady," he formally addressed her. "I believe I have the honour of having this dance with you."

"Indeed you have," and she rose from her chair and slid her arm into William's as they walked to the dance floor.

No sooner had William escorted Amelia back to her seat after the first dance when another admirer requested the pleasure. She was festooned with dance requests, much to William's chagrin, and he watched her expertly negotiate the steps of the strathspeys and reels as she danced with a variety of partners. He chose only a few, and trying to put the information about John aside, attempted to look animated throughout the evening. Amelia, on the other hand, exuded happiness, but it was not towards anybody there. She was imagining dancing with John and how handsome he would look in the matching outfit William was wearing. In popular demand, her dance card became full with a variety of men eager to partner her but, no matter who she was dancing with, she kept wishing it was John she was partnering. But she had a delightful social evening. During the break she spoke to many people whom she knew - her ladies from the art class and others she had met in people's homes and at the recitals. William on the other hand, had a fleeting melancholic moment when the break was announced. That was when he had intended taking Amelia outside to ask for her hand. He would, he told himself, have to be patient and wait. At least he had the last dance, another minuet, and when they reached the point in the dance where they had to step towards one another William tilted his head towards her and said, "You really are the belle of the ball this evening Amelia."

"That's nice. Thank you William." The dance continued until once more they stepped towards one another.

"Your father has asked me to spend Christmas with you at the estate. So I will have the pleasure of your company then."

"Oh," she said, surprised, and turned her head to smile at an acquaintance nearby. The dancing between them continued in silence until the music stopped. "Thank you Amelia. It was a pleasure to dance with you," William said as he escorted her back to the table. "I hope there will be many more." Her father and brother were at the table.

"Well my dear," Lord Hugh addressed his daughter. "You certainly looked as though you enjoyed yourself this evening."

"Yes I did. Thank you father."

"And what a good dancer you are Amelia," William enthusiastically told her, and, wanting her father to know his intentions, added, "As I said. I hope there will be many more with you." Amelia responded with a curt smile.

"And so," announced Lord High rising from his seat. "It is time to leave."

William immediately said, "I have booked the carriage for you."

"Oh. Very kind of you William," Lord Hugh responded.

"William and I are going to a club for a few drinks," Malcolm told them. "I'll make my own way back."

"Very well," responded his father.

As they were leaving, William called out to Malcom, "I'll be back in a moment."

Once outside William assisted Amelia up the steps of the carriage followed by her father who turned to William and said, "We look forward to seeing you again soon. Don't we Amelia?"

"Yes father," she meekly responded.

"I wish you good night William."

"Good night to you both sir," William replied, giving them a wave as the carriage drew away.

"It was a delightful evening," Amelia told her father as they made their short journey home.

"I'm so glad you enjoyed the ball my dear. You looked wonderful. And you and William looked a perfect couple on the floor. He really was very attentive towards you this evening. Don't you think?"

"Yes father. He certainly was."

"You know, I have a feeling he is going to propose."

Amelia gasped. "Surely not."

Ignoring her comment her father continued, "I, for one, would be delighted if he did. He's a fine fellow."

Amelia couldn't respond. She longed to tell her father about John, but couldn't.

"You're being very quiet my dear."

" Yes," she replied. "My mind was elsewhere."

"Well my dear. We'll see what happens."

The carriage arrived at their door and Amelia stepped down without saying a word until Benjamin answered the door.

"I'm going to retire father. I'm exhausted after all that dancing."

"I'm sure you are my dear. And I'm so glad you enjoyed yourself this evening."

She glided up the stairs where Meg was ready to greet her. "So," Meg excitedly asked, "How wis it?"

"It was a lovely evening," Amelia nonchallantly answered walking towards her bedchamber.

"And ye danced wi' William?" she enquired.

"Yes. Three times actually," Amelia wistfully responded. "But," she added "there were many more admirers, so I'm feeling rather tired."

"Aye of course," said Meg, and discerning her mistress's pensive mood she desisted from asking any more questions.

Amelia hadn't wanted to confide in Meg her musings at the ball, preferring to keep her loving thoughts of John to herself till she retired.

When William, in a slightly drunken state, retired to his bedchamber he too was thinking of John, but certainly not in the same light as Amelia. He had been flabbergasted when he realised the link to Lord Hugh's gamekeeper, for whom his lordship had great respect. And of course he couldn't speak a word of it to Malcolm who was commenting at the club on how attentive he was towards Amelia at the ball. But now, as he lay in his bed, he contemplated the competition and the best course of action to be rid of this man. The perspective had now changed with the revelation he had a link to the family. He couldn't possibly trump up charges now. And what to do if he wasn't involved in any illicit printing? Jock was convinced he wasn't. And it was too cold to ask Jock to hang around for hours monitoring the man's every movement. But the worst of his dilemma was the fact he was starting to fall in love with Amelia. She looked bewitching at the ball and he could feel anger mounting towards this man called John. Still, he reasoned, nothing could be done until Jock had thoroughly investigated him. He would tell him to follow the man called Alec one evening and see where he went and that, he concluded, might on a whisper of a chance, lead to something.

XV

John noticed Amelia's self-assured expression as she strode into the coffee house.

"You're looking very pleased with yourself," he told her as she settled into her chair.

"Yes. I do feel good," she responded.

"For any particular reason?"

"You mean other than seeing you," she smiled. "It was an interesting weekend."

"How was the ball?"

"It was a delightful evening. But," she replied in a pensive tone, "I was thinking about you all the time and imagining us dancing together."

He looked adoringly at her and commented, "You must have looked beautiful."

"Yes," she replied in a dismissive tone. "William was rather attentive towards me."

"William?" John asked, trying to subdue any jealousy he felt.

"Yes. You know, my brother's friend. Father thinks he's going to propose soon."

"Propose!" exclaimed John.

"Yes," she replied matter-of-factly. "Father and Malcolm have been trying to persuade me for a while to have him as my suitor"

"And?" John anxiously asked.

"John, I have no intention of marrying him," she firmly stated. "But I have to accept the reality. It will get awkward. Father has asked him to spend Christmas with us at the estate and he's made it quite plain he would be delighted if I accepted the proposal. He thinks he's a fine chap."

John could feel his anxiety mounting. "But," replied John, trying to reassure himself, "nothing has happened yet."

"No," she responded in a perfectly calm manner. "But I'm quite sure he's going to ask me over the Christmas period."

"Oh Amelia," he said in a constrained tone. "Are you sure you won't accept?"

"Of course I won't," she firmly replied. "It's you I love. Not William."

"But if he does propose, you'll get a lot of pressure from your father and your brother to accept it."

"Yes. I expect I will. But John, you know me well enough, I'm not going to enter into something as important as marriage just to suit them. I have to do what I want to do."

"But Amelia, they could be very persuasive." He lowered his eyes.

She reassuringly touched his arm and said, "You mustn't worry John. It's you I love. That won't change."

John took a moment to compose himself, then clasping his hands on his knees he looked at her and adopted as calm an expression as he could muster and said, "You must do what you think is right. You must consider the type of future you want." He paused and, after a moment, continued in a restrained voice, "I have to say it would be difficult for me if you thought it best to marry William …"

"But," she whispered, "it's you I love."

"Let me continue," John said in a sombre tone. "This is important. If you do choose to marry William, I would understand. He has better prospects than I. And," he stoically continued, "I will have the grace to accept your decision."

"John," she whispered. "I adore you. I'm not going to marry William."

"Aye. I hear what you're saying. But you must consider it seriously. For how can we carry on? Of course I want to spend more time with you, but we move in difference circles. How can they ever blend?"

"Love surpasses all," Amelia smiled radiantly at him. And John responded.

"I have to go." She quickly rose from her chair. "Please write."

"I will," he replied as he wistfully watched her depart and wondered what their future might be.

Before Amelia departed, Jock was walking briskly down South Bridge en route to William's for their meeting. He saw a sedan waiting outside John's coffee house and, curious to know who the chairmen were waiting for, he glanced inside and saw John and Amelia. He didn't dally so as not to be late. William was punctilious about punctuality. He arrived on time and immediately narrated the latest news.

"I went tae his lodgings early ivery mornin'. He kept tae his routine, gaun oot at ten tae eight ...but on Friday, instead o' coming oot of his close, he came oot o' Blackfriars Street. The street opposite."

"Oh," remarked William. "What was he doing there I wonder?"

"That wis the only untoward thing that happened. Except, I've jist seen him in John's coffee house. He wis with yon lady."

"Another assignation," William mumbled under his breath. "Now," he firmly addressed Jock. "I tell you what you have to do. Find out where this Alec has his printing place. It cannot be too difficult for you – you've got good investigative skills. Spend the next day or so making enquiries about him and do your best to find out if he's the one printing the hand bills. Also, check how many printing establishments there are around the Blackfriars Street area. There can't be that many and it's a small profession. They mostly know one another, so they should know who this Alec is. But be careful to be very discreet. This is just between you and me. Is that clear Jock?"

"Aye sir," replied Jock.

"Very good. Once you've located where Alec works, try your best to find out if he's involved in the handbills. Then, I want you to go to the lodgings very early, maybe six in the morning. I know, you'll be cold. I'll give you some extra money to buy a good plaid. But if John was coming up Blackfriars Street, there is every likelihood he was coming from a printer's nearby. I realise this is pure conjecture, but that could be why he doesn't linger in taverns. He's exhausted doing extra shifts." He paused. "Apart from that Friday morning, is there anything else untoward about his movements?"

"Naw. He goes tae work. Does his shift. Sees his caddy friend a few nights in various taverns. Oh," he paused, "and there are notes bein' passed."

"Definitely between this lady and him?"

"Oh aye. I've been keeping a check on that." Jock noticed William's expression change to one of fury.

"I want these meetings to be monitored. Is that clear?" William told him.

"Aye sir," Jock meekly responded.

"Right Jock. Your task is to find Alec. Follow the McCulloch man constantly, morning and night and I'll pay you well. Forget about our Monday meetings just drop a daily note in my pigeon hole with your progress and if I want to see you I'll leave instructions for you."

"Right sir," said Jock. "There's a big meeting at Lawrie's Rooms this Wednesday. Muir is going tae be elected Vice-President of the Associated Friends of the People. If John doesn't appear tae be going tae the meeting, dae ye want me still tae attend?"

"Difficult decision," William replied, then paused. "Yes. I want you to be there. We have to start gathering evidence about Muir's seditious behaviour."

"Right sir. I'll be in touch," said Jock, accepting the three guineas William handed him. "That's very generous sir."

"I want you to do a good job. Find the connection between this John and illicit printing. And give me the progress of the meetings with the lady."

When Jock left he wondered why William was so interested in these meetings. They had nothing to do with illicit printing. Curious, he thought he would investigate further.

John, of course, was quite oblivious to William's shenanigans and, although Peter had warned him to watch his back, he was so caught up in his love for Amelia, he quite forgot about any danger. He continued as before, helping Alec produce handbills but not as frequently as he did in the beginning as his focus had now altered to Amelia. It was very unsettling hearing about William's forthcoming proposal. And although she did say she loved him, as he returned to his humble lodgings, and in the small hours, surveyed his spartan space with only room for a pallet bed, his small wooden box and two wooden pegs affixed to the back of the door which sufficed for his meagre wardrobe, he began to feel despondent. How could he possibly provide for her? Mr Brechin appreciated his hard work but there was no hope of promotion for at least another two years. Maybe he could go back to the land become a gamekeeper, like his father? When he returned home at Christmas he would ask his advice as to how he could follow in his father's footsteps. Meanwhile, he would write to his love, and if Peter didn't have the time to deliver the notes, he could employ a boy to run his errands. He just had to hope her love for him was strong, because he was quite sure her father and brother would do everything to persuade her to marry William. He hoped with all his heart, as he told her in the note, that she would be resistant to their exhortations. But he didn't want to put pressure on her, and he would respect her decision if she chose William to please her family.

She immediately replied assuring him there would never be anybody else. 'I love you with all my heart,' she wrote. 'It is a blessing about William's proposal because it has meant I have had to think long and hard about my future and I realise, with such a certainty, that I want it to be spent with you. I can hardly believe the joy I feel when I am with you. It is quite overwhelming. Let us luxuriate in our correspondence and the few moments we are able to spend together and then, if and when the time comes, I will tell father and persuade him we should be together. I am going to St Cecilia's Hall on Friday. A sedan will be waiting for me when the recital finishes, maybe we could catch a glimpse of one another then? All my love Amelia.'

'I have an idea my beloved,' John wrote. 'I shall get two silver lockets engraved with the inscription 'love you forever'. I can wear mine in my breast pocket next to my heart, as you could do with yours. We shall then always be together."

XVI

Jock began by enquiring about Alec in a variety of taverns. These became packed when the shops closed at eight and the tradesmen spent, predictably, the next two hours sipping ale until the drum of the Town Guard sounded at ten to warn residents of the deluge of human waste to be hurled onto the streets. He had no joy the first night but the following evening he decided to go to the White Horse in the Canongate. As he entered the busy tavern and looked at the faces in the crowd, he recognised a man he had seen at the meeting in Lawrie's Rooms. Under the pretext of attracting the wench's attention for a tankard of ale, he achieved both his objectives and stood beside the stranger.

He addressed the man. "It's a bitter night, is it no?"

"Aye. It is that," the man replied. "It's guid it's busy here. Keeps us a' warm fur nothing."

Jock chuckled. "Aye. That's true. Whit is it ye dae?"

"I work at the Flesh Market an' I look forward tae ma tankard o' ale, or a few after work," he chuckled. "An' whit dae ye dae?"

Jock had his stock answer ready. "I dae errands fur a gentleman. He pays well."

"Weel. That's the main thing," the man said.

"I'm working late this evening," Jock paused. "I wis wondering. Wud ye ken a guid printer? Ma gentleman," he lowered his voice, "who is a part o' the movement, is looking fur a good printer because he wis thinking o' writing a novel. "

"Oh," the man responded enthusiastically, "I ken someone. He's called Alec. He works fur Peter Williamson, the bookseller at the Luckenbooths. He's a reputation fur being a guid printer, an' novels ur his trade."

"That sounds interesting. Whaur does he work frae?" Jock nonchalantly asked.

"Somewhere in the Cowgate, I think."

"Ony address?"

"Na." Then the man looked animated. "Bit ye can see him at the meeting the morra nicht at Lawrie's. He'll be there. An' he aye goes tae the White Hart efter."

"Thanks," replied Jock. He quickly finished his drink. "I hae tae go. I'm meeting up wi' a freend."

"Guid to hae met ye. Nae doubt see ye at a meeting. I cannae gang tae the meeting th'morro nicht but I'll see ye at yin o' them."

"Aye," replied Jock and pushed his way to the exit. After the warmth of the tavern it took a moment to acclimatise to the bitter night, exacerbated as it was by a strong wind coming down the Canongate, but he wrapped his plaid effectively round his body and started to briskly stride up the hill to lessen the impact of the cold. He was pleased with his progress and would report to William once he had discovered where Alec worked.

Rising before six the following morning, he waited patiently for John to emerge from his lodgings, grateful for the extra money William had given him to purchase another plaid. At ten to eight, John emerged and proceeded up the hill to his work. After his shift, Jock followed him to the meeting at Lawrie's rooms in the Lawnmarket. The place was packed, with barely enough room to move. He watched John weave his way across the crowd to join Alec.

In the opening address by the chairman, a man he didn't recognise, he discovered the reason it was so packed. "Friends," the chairman said. "We welcome Delegates from the Societies of the Friends of the People, in and around Edinburgh, who are gathered here this evening." He paused. "And it is agreed that the two resolutions on the motions proposed by Captain Johnston at the last sitting, be re-published in all the Edinburgh and Glasgow newspapers. The first resolution: 'That the name or names of any person or persons, belonging to the Associated Friends of the People, who may be found guilty of rioting, or creating or aiding sedition or tumult, shall be expunged from the books of the society.'

The other motion resolved is: 'Any person acting properly who may be persecuted or oppressed by the arm of power, shall be protected by the whole societies.'" He paused and looked to his left where Thomas Muir was seated and announced: "Friends, we have great pleasure in unanimously electing Thomas Muir of Huntershill as Vice-President of the Associated Friends of the People. He will say a few words."

"Thank you," said Muir, as he rose from his chair. "A warm welcome to you all." He looked round the room and addressing the earnest faces said: "Friends, I consider the cause of parliamentary reform to be essential to the salvation of my country. And the movement for reform is gathering encouraging momentum and I am confident we shall succeed in our demands to restore the freedom of election and an equal representation of the people in Parliament. And Friends, this is a national movement. At the recent annual dinner held in London by the Constitutional Whig revolutionists, they stressed the importance of the liberty of the press resolving to have a speedy annihilation of every government that shrinks from investigation. And as you know, Captain Johnston has now launched the *Edinburgh Gazette*er whose articles will counter those written by the government sponsored Edinburgh Herald and other such papers." He paused. "And from afar, the French government have decided that France would spare no expense to support a Republican insurrection in Scotland and also in Ireland.

Lastly, we shall be holding a three day convention – the first of many it is hoped – with one hundred and sixty delegates who will represent eighty parliamentary reform societies from thirty-five Scottish towns and villages. The Convention of delegates of the Associated Friends of the People will be held in Laurie's room, James's Court. Colonel Dalrymple will be in the chair, aided by Lord Daer. I conclude now by saying – Friends, knowledge must always precede reformation, and who shall dare to say that the people should be debarred from information. Sleep in a state is always followed by servitude. And this Friends, is the path we seek to avoid in our efforts to create a venerable democratic society." As he sat down, the crowd erupted in loud cheers and clapping of hands at his words of wisdom. Even Jock was impressed by his eloquence, honed as it was by years as an advocate at the bar.

The chairman then rose. "We thank you Mr Muir for your sage words. We must hold fast to our beliefs and we shall overcome the wrath of those who attempt to deny our demands and succeed in our quest for universal suffrage." At that, the room resounded to loud cries of 'Aye!' When the noise had died down, Jock, wanting to be accompanied by someone when he left the meeting so as not to look conspicuous, asked the man next to him, "Are ye gaun tae the White Hart?"

"Oh aye" the man heartily responded. "We hae tae celebrate Thomas Muir an' a' the work he does fur the cause."

"Aye," agreed Jock, and as he noticed John and Alec leaving the room, quickly added, "I'll git ye an ale." Delighted the man replied, "Very guid."

Once outside, Jock made sure they were several men behind John and Alec and when they got to the thriving inn, he positioned himself to ensure Alec was in his vision when he sat in the back room to take his ale amongst the others. After a short while he saw both Alec and John rise from their chairs and he quickly finished off his ale, bade the man good night and went outside to hide in a doorway. A few minutes later they emerged and both walked towards the Cowgate. But when they reached Niddry Street, John took a left. Alec however carried on until he reached the next close on the right. When he turned into Robertson Close Jock hid behind the side of a building and observed Alec entering a door half way up on the right hand side. He waited some considerable time in the shadows but as Alec didn't reappear, he decided to walk stealthily up the close to see where he could possibly be. He stopped outside the entrance Alec had gone into and looked carefully up at the building. If there was a printing room, because of the weight of the equipment, it was highly likely it was on the ground floor, where he was standing. He noticed a tiny opening in the drawn wooden shutters, and glancing round to check if anyone was about, peered into the crack. Although his vision was minimal he could discern it was not a domestic environment as he espied the printing press. He was delighted with the discovery, as he was sure William would be also.

Thursday morning and evening were no different than other days with John. He went to work, saw Peter, received a note and went back to his lodgings early. On Friday, arriving at his usual six o'clock hour nearby John's lodgings and, anticipating an uneventful freezing two hours, he was brought to his senses when he saw John leaving his lodgings at six thirty and cross over to Blackfriars Street. Still dark, with a thick smoky haze in the air, Jock was able to follow him undetected to the foot of Blackfriars Street where he turned right, crossed over and into Robertson Close and entered the same door as Alec had. If John was helping Alec, he presumed he would have to wait at least an hour in the freezing cold and he felt he deserved the generous amount of money William was giving him. John emerged at seven thirty and made his way up Niddry Street, en route to his work. But when he arrived at the Luckenbooths Jock observed him going into a Silversmiths. He was there until five to eight when he emerged and went to start his shift. All this he would relate to William as he said in his note suggesting they have a meeting at five o'clock.

They were seated while Jock was relating the latest news but it was only when he got to the point where John went to Alec's that William reacted. He leapt out of his chair and ecstatically exclaimed, "We've got him!" He started to pace. "But… we need evidence. You now have to assiduously follow Alec. If they are printing these hand-bills, I want tangible proof. I want you to witness Alec distributing them. If, of course, he is. But I am sure I am right." He heartily shook Jock's hand. "Well done. What wonderful news. You richly deserve being well paid."

"Thank ye sir. Oh. Jist yin ither thing," Jock remarked. "It wis odd. Bit before work he went intae a silversmith's in ane o' the Luckenbooths…"

"Silversmith's!" exclaimed William.

"Aye. He wis there fur quite a while."

"What in God's name was he doing there? Can you find out?"

"It wud be difficult. It's usually a personal thing that people gang tae Silversmiths fur."

William sounded agitated. "Exactly."

"And there hae been mair notes passed." William looked furious. He was silent for a moment and then reso-lutely told Jock, "You must trail Alec. That's a priority. Understood? And let me know the moment you have news." He started to pace. "I think we've got him," he mumbled. "And working in that cesspit of humanity in the Cowgate seems an apt place for a scoundrel like that. Right Jock, you may go." He handed him three guineas.

"I await with baited breath your forthcoming news. I'm tied up all day Monday till five but we can meet here soon after."

"Very well sir. Thank ye," and he turned and left.

What Jock didn't mention to William was the fact he had that afternoon started to make enquiries about the lady. He couldn't fathom why William was so interested in the meetings and he wanted to find out more about this lady who lived at eighty-one Queen Street. He discovered she was Lord Robertson's daughter. Her name was Amelia and she had a brother who was an advocate. Jock thought he would investigate further on the Saturday and ask a few caddies if they had any more information.

XVII

Jock did find a caddie who was familiar with the names of the advocates and when he asked about Lord Robertson's son the caddie immediately said, "Aye. Malcolm Robertson. He works wi' William Gilchrist in the High Court." And to Jock's surprise he added, "They're guid friends." So, there is an interesting connection thought Jock. However, he had more important things to think about and that evening he had followed William's orders and kept close watch on Alec whose favourite haunt, he had discovered, was the Beehive Inn.

He arrived at the Inn early evening, ordered a tankard of ale and waited. True to his informer's word, Alec came in a while later and started talking to friends until nine, when Jock saw him downing his ale and wishing his friends good night. When he left the Inn, he proceeded to walk in the direction of the Cowgate - to his printing room Jock presumed. And he was right. He waited some time in the shadows to ascertain Alec was ensconced in his work, then once more peered through the crack in the shutters. This time he could hear the handle of the press being turned. He retreated back to the shadows and waited.

Alec left the printing room minutes before the Town Guard beat the drum to herald the deposit of wastes, and subsequent sluicing. Ducking and diving to avoid being caught in the hurling of the wastes, he followed Alec to the High Street where he witnessed him attach a handbill to a Public notice board. The following day was the Sabbath and he couldn't contact William then, but he would make a point of dropping a note off first thing Monday morning saying they had to have a meeting at five thirty.

"So what have you got?" William eagerly asked Jock the moment he arrived.

"I saw Alec putting up a handbill on the High Street at ten on Saturday nicht," Jock proudly told him.

William gleefully clasped his hands. "Well done Jock. That is wonderful news," he exclaimed and started to pace. "We can now arrest John McCulloch for his involvement in these seditious acts. It is too late to contact Sheriff Pringle, but I will do so first thing in the morning and arrange for the arrest at his work," he triumphantly proclaimed. "Very good work Jock. You can take two well- earned days off after which we will start to monitor Thomas Muir in earnest." He then stood beside Jock and said, "We must keep a close watch on this three day Convention next week. I am quite convinced we shall soon have enough evidence to find Muir guilty of the wicked practices of advising persons to purchase Paine's 'Rights of Man' – a seditious publication. It is calculated to produce a spirit of disloyalty, and … disaffection to the King and Government. Muir has to be stopped. So Jock, that is our next task."

"Very well sir."

"And I shall pay you handsomely for your good work," and he handed Jock four guineas."

"That's too much sir," Jock protested.

"Indeed it is not," William emphatically told him. "You have accomplished what I had set out to do and that was to find John McCulloch guilty of seditious illicit practices. I am very grateful to you;"

"Thank ye sir. I'm glad ye're satisfied wi' ma services."

"I am indeed Jock," William assured him. "And we shall see one another at seven in two days' time."

"Richt sir," and Jock took his leave.

St Giles clock chimed the half hour as Jock stepped onto the High Street. He started to saunter down the hill, reflecting on William's alleged good friendship with Amelia's brother. Despite being handsomely paid by William, Jock thought William arrogant, and he still smarted at his riff-raff comment. Then he started to question the reason for William's determination to ensure McCulloch's arrest. And despite the fact it had been Alec who had put up the handbill, William had not even mentioned that he too should also be arrested. It was as if he was obsessed with McCulloch and his obsession bordered on the irrational. And then it dawned on Jock. William was jealous. He had designs on his friend Malcolm's sister! McCulloch was his rival, and Jock knew William well enough to know he could not cope with being usurped by anyone. And McCulloch's arrest was therefore a convenient way to get a rival removed and successfully blemish his character and future opportunities.

He had by this time reached South Bridge and, having nothing else planned, he decided to go to John's coffee shop and, hopefully, witness another meeting between John and Amelia. He did.

John was already seated, facing the door, when Jock arrived. He gave his order to the boy, picked up a newspaper, and sat nearby hoping to catch snippets of their conversation. He heard the door opening and saw John's face transform into one of unadulterated happiness. When Amelia walked over to join him Jock glanced at her expression. She too, looked overjoyed to see him.

John was so engrossed in her company, he was oblivious to others in the coffee house which was useful for Jock. As he observed them interacting with one another he realised they were indeed in love. And her exclamation of delight when John produced a small box and retrieved a tiny silver locket was only further confirmation. Glancing periodically at the couple, Jock sat deliberating about what he should do. John was engaged in criminal activity but, he told himself, he did have a conscience. Could he be party to destroying the lives of two people who loved one another purely to satisfy William's jealous wrath? He made a decision. He would do something good in his life. He would find John's caddie friend and get him to warn John that he was to be arrested in the morning.

He rose, paid for his coffee, and rushed up the High Street to where the caddies congregated. He didn't know Peter's name but he asked the group of they knew which caddie was friendly with a man who worked at the *Cale-*

donian Mercury. They conferred with each other and decided it was Peter.

"Dae ye ken whaur he is?" Jock urgently asked.

"He's got the nicht aff," one of the caddies told him. "He'll be in a tavern maist likely."

"Which yin?" implored Jock. "It's urgent."

"He coud be in ony yin," the man casually replied.

Jock spent over an hour searching in taverns asking if anyone had seen a caddie called Peter and was eventually told he was likely to be at the White Horse. Jock ran down the hill into the tavern and scoured the faces for that of Peter. Seeing him in conversation with someone, he immediately went up to him. "I've got a bit o' urgent news fur ye," he told Peter breathlessly. "Ye hae tae come ootdoors." Bemused, Peter followed him and once in the cold night air Jock told him. "Yer friend John is gaun tae be arrestit in the morning."

"How dae ye ken?" Peter anxiously asked.

"I jist dae," Jock replied curtly. "Ye maun find him an' warn him. He'll hae tae leave the city." Jock put his hand in his pocket, retrieved the guineas William had given him and handed them to Peter. "Gie him this. He'll need it."

"Stranger," Peter replied. "Why are ye daein' this?"

"Fur ma conscience," Jock soberly retorted. "It'll mak' me feel better. Jist find him."

"I will," said Peter and, as he started to dash up the hill to John's lodgings, Jock called out, "It's William Gilchrist whae's dun it!"

Peter thumped loudly on the MacFadyen door. He heard footsteps approaching from within and the door was smartly opened by Mr MacFadyen. "Why the noise?" he curtly asked. "Whit is it ye want?"

"I hae tae speak tae John," Peter urgently told him.

"He's in his room," Mr MacFadyen said, and as Peter stepped into the narrow hall, John emerged from his box room.

Surprised, John exclaimed, "Peter. Whit are ye doing here at this time?"

"I hae tae speak tae ye," and he went over and ushered John quickly into his room and shut the door and breathlessly blurted out, "Ye'r gaun tae be arrestit in the morning."

"Whit!"

"Aye. I've jist been told by a man who came tae the White Horse tae find me." He hurriedly continued, "A wis at the port the day. There's a sloop bound fer Waalhaven fer a cargo o' Dutch cheese. I ken the Captain. Jist tell him ye're a friend o' mine. He'll tak a passenger…"

"Whit? A sloop?" John anxiously asked.

"Aye," Peter spluttered. "A single masted sail boat wi' a jib. It'll be a rough crossing this time o' year. Bit," he hastily added, "ye cannae stay here" and glanced at his watch. "It'll be leaving on the high tide in an hour. At eleven. It's the Peggy Lee an' it's at Berth six. Quick. Git yer bag."

Stunned, John exclaimed, "Anither country?"

"Aye. Ye cannae stay here. Ye've nae choice."

"I must let Amelia ken," he replied and, retrieving paper, pen and ink, began: "Dearest, by the time you receive this note I will have left. Peter has been told I am to be arrested in the morning. I have no choice but to go. A man told Peter it was William Gilchrist who has done this. At eleven tonight, I board a boat for Waalhaven but I shall contact you somehow. And my dearest, I shall wear the locket in my breast pocket, next to my heart, until we be reunited some day. All my love. John."

He handed the note to Peter and hastily wrote another to his parents which Peter agreed to make sure it reached them. Then, grabbing his bag and a few belongings, he opened the door and rushed out the house calling out to the MacFadyens. "Thank ye fur kindness. I hae tae gang"

Once onto the street, Peter handed him the guineas Jock had given him. "The man telt me tae gie this tae ye. He said, ye'll need it." And from another pocket he gave John all the money he had.

"I cannae tak' that," John protested.

"Aye. Ye can. Gie a guinea tae the Captain. That'll take ye there."

"An' the note?" said John anxiously.

"Dinnae worry, I'll get it tae her" Peter responded and heartily shook his friend's hand. "We will meet agin. I hae nae doubt aboot that. Guid luck ma freend." And so they parted company - John to the Port of Leith, Peter to Amelia's.

XVIII

There was a hard frost on the ground but Peter tried his best to get to Queen Street as quickly as he could. He was flustered when he arrived at the house to hand in the note and pulled hard on the bell. When Benjamin answered the door he heard Meg's voice call from within. "Is that a note fur Miss Amelia?"

"Aye. It is. Rather late in the day though," Benjamin disdainfully commented and partially closed the front door.

"Is that for me?" Peter discerned Amelia call out.

"Aye. It is m'am," Benjamin assured her, and Peter could hear the rustling of her dress as she hurried down the stairs to receive it. A moment later, he heard a grief-stricken moan then Meg shouting, "Miss Amelia hae fainted! Quick Benjamin! Git the smelling salts."

Peter, distressed at hearing Amelia's response to the note and not wanting to intrude on the outcome of the news, quietly left and made his way to the High Street all the while wondering what would become of it all.

Back in the house, pandemonium had erupted. Lord Hugh rushed out of his study in his nightgown and was half way down the stairs, followed hastily by Malcolm, by the time Meg was administering the smelling salts. "What in God's name has happened?" he anxiously asked.

"Miss Amelia fainted sir," Meg frantically replied.

Beside himself with concern, he asked, "What on earth has caused her such distress?"

"It's the note sir," she hastily told him.

"What's written in the note?" But, as Amelia had clutched the note to her breast, they were oblivious as to the content that had caused her to react in such a dramatic manner.

"Shall I git a damp cloth tae wipe her forehead?" asked Meg.

"Yes. Yes," Lord Hugh abruptly responded. "And quick."

Equally concerned, Malcolm asked his father, "What can I do?"

"Lift her up, and take her to the drawing room," he replied.

Malcolm bent down and as he gently lifted up her limp body, the muscles in her hand relaxed and the note fluttered to the flagstone floor. His father picked up the note, read it as Malcolm proceeded to carry her up the stairs and exclaimed, "Oh my God. Amelia was having a secret liaison with a criminal."

"What!" Malcolm exclaimed.

"Someone called John." But as they were entering the drawing room, Lord Hugh tempered his anger and said, "She's still in a state of shock. We must handle this with care." And, still holding the note, he stretched out his hand to let Malcolm read it. Once done, he forcefully added, "It is incredible. My daughter having a liaison with a criminal."

Meg came rushing into the room and, as Malcolm laid his sister out on a chaise longue, immediately knelt on the floor beside her and began to soothe her forehead with a damp cloth. Lord Hugh and Malcolm hovered over Meg as she ministered to her mistress. After a few minutes

Amelia started to regain consciousness and realised her hand was no longer clutching the note. Immediately her expression changed to one of panic. "Where is the note?" she exclaimed as she attempted to sit up.

"I have it here," her father sternly responded, holding the note in his outstretched hand.

Dismayed, Amelia slumped back into a prone position and started to sob.

Malcolm began to get impatient. "We have to question her," he told his father.

"I know," his father responded. "Of course we do, but … wait a moment."

But Malcolm was not so generous hearted. "Meg. Could you leave us."

"Of course sir," she said, rising to her feet and hastily leaving the room. When the door was closed Malcolm bluntly asked Amelia, "Who is this criminal you have been liaising with Amelia? We want answers. Now."

"Yes, Amelia," her father sternly asked. "Who is the man?"

Amelia responded with heart wrenching sobs. "It's John!" she wailed.

Father and son looked at one another, bemused, then a flash of recognition crossed Lord Hugh's face and he exclaimed, "John McCulloch!"

Stunned. Malcolm cried out, "Not the gamekeeper's son?"

"And he's gone!" Amelia wailed.

Furious Malcolm said, "Because he's a criminal."

"He is not a criminal," she protested.

"William," her brother emphatically responded, "would not arrange the arrest of someone unless he had concrete evidence. I know him well enough for that."

"Oh Malcolm," she implored, "I couldn't help falling in love with him."

"Of course you could," he dismissively responded. "What a ridiculous notion. Did you think a life of penury would be romantic?"

"It just happened Malcolm," she immediately interjected. "It was completely unexpected. But …I've never felt such joy in my life," and her face lit up with radiance.

"I'm not interested in that in the slightest," Malcolm promptly responded. "What," he demanded, "was he being arrested for?"

Amelia's expression altered to one of concern. She lowered her eyes, and in a quiet, hesitant voice replied. "Printing handbills," she sobbed, "for the reform movement."

"Printing seditious handbills!" Malcolm exploded. "Of course that's a criminal offence…"

"What a fool!" Lord Hugh interjected. "How can you love someone who is prepared to commit a criminal offence?"

"And a serious one at that," Malcolm promptly added. Then he remembered the note, glanced at the clock. It was ten twenty. "I have a carriage outside. I was supposed to meet William, but no matter …I may still be able to stop McCulloch" and he quickly turned towards the door.

"Don't go," Amelia pleaded. "I don't want John harmed."

Malcolm turned as he about the leave the room and abruptly told her, "If William thinks he is a danger to society and has arranged for his arrest and he's absconding, then he is a fugitive," and he stormed out of the room, sped down the stairs and out of the door to a waiting carriage. As there was a hard frost on the ground when Malcolm got into the carriage he knew the horses would not be able to canter because of it, but nevertheless urged the driver, "Quick as you can. Port of Leith."

There was a brief silence in the drawing room when Malcolm left, until Lord Hugh, standing rigid beside Amelia, barely concealing his fury, spoke to her and said sternly, "I am disappointed in you Amelia. The daughter, whom I raised to be a lady, consorting with a criminal. It is beyond belief."

"Father. Don't be cruel. Please," she begged him. "It's not like that. I tried so hard, so often to rid myself of this passion. But the more I tried to deny it, the worse it became. I love John. I really do. And there is nothing I can do about it. He truly is the love of my life. I know it."

"But Amelia. He is a criminal," her father firmly stated.

She lowered her eyes, dimmed her voice and said, "I may have encouraged him."

Shocked, her father furiously responded, "What do you mean? Encouraged him to engage in criminal activities?"

"No," she hastily added. "But he knew I felt proud of him helping the Reform movement."

"And look at the consequences," her father immediately retorted. "He is now labelled a criminal."

"Labelled by William," Amelia quietly responded, then, raising herself up to a sitting position, she calmly announced, "I don't know how William found out, but I think he arranged for John to be arrested because he was jealous of him."

"Don't be ridiculous Amelia," her father angrily retorted. "William was having him arrested because he was committing a criminal offence."

"But many people in the city are printing handbills," she quickly replied, and told him emphatically, "I am quite convinced William did it to get rid of John."

"Of course he wouldn't have done that," her father replied in an indignant tone. "What a fanciful idea. William is a decent man."

"No father. I am quite convinced he did it out of spite. He is in love with me. I got the impression, like you, he was going to propose at the ball. But I was glad he didn't because I could only think of John when we were there."

"Well I would be happy if you married William," her father immediately responded.

"But I don't love him father," Amelia emphatically insisted. "I love John. Not William."

"But he would make a far better suitor…."

"But I don't want to spend my life with William. I want to spend it with John…"

"That also is fanciful. John, unless Malcolm stops him, is having to flee arrest. And if he does escape, you may never see him again. He would be branded a fugitive. He may never be able to return."

On hearing that Amelia started to sob. "I couldn't bear the thought of never seeing him again. I love him. And he loves me. I can't imagine life without him."

Her father was confused as to how he should respond. His daughter in love with a criminal! He couldn't countenance that. But he remembered how he had liked John and recommended him to Mr Brechin because he thought John a decent young man. What a dilemma. But he also then remembered the love he felt for his beloved Margaret, and knew how difficult it was to quell true love. He truly understood his daughter's distress. He softened his tone in an endeavour to assuage her sorrow. "Amelia," he began, "I can see how affected you are by this, but you are young. You are bound to meet other young men…"

"But they won't understand me as John does," she earnestly replied.

"Maybe. But you have to think of your future," her father stoically responded. "Your reality. John is now labelled a criminal."

"By William," she hastily added.

"We will never know if that is the case …"

"I know he did it. And I never want to see William in this house, ever again."

"That's harsh Amelia. He is Malcolm's best friend."

"I don't care if he is. I will never speak to him again." Her face full of anguish she told him, "I will wait for John's return," then burst into heartrending, grief-stricken sobs.

On seeing his beloved daughter in such a state, he was overcome with compassion. He lifted her up and embraced her in an attempt to quell her despair.

Lord Hugh was still solicitously comforting his daughter when Malcolm's carriage arrived at the docks. "Stop the cab!" he shouted to the driver, and rushed over to the daily schedule of sailings listed on a board at the entrance. He quickly scoured the details. 'Peggy Lee, Waalhaven, eleven pm. Berth six.' Malcolm looked at his watch. Five minutes to go. "Berth Six!" he shouted to the driver. "Fast as you can."

The carriage reached the quayside … just as the main sail on the Peggy Lee was being hoisted at the mouth of the port. John – standing on deck – was looking out to the dark horizon and pondering an uncertain future.

EPILOGUE

The Captain had numerous contacts at the harbour. He exchanged John's guineas for gilders and quickly secured him lodgings and work as a shiploader. It was a start. And using Peter as an intermediary the Captain agreed to take and collect letters from Amelia. Through their intermittent correspondence their love for one another remained constant and after a period of five years, Lord Hugh finally relented and agreed to their marriage. John left Holland, returned to Scotland and their marriage took place in the chapel on the estate, where John was appointed assistant Manager.

The threat of John's arrest on his return had been erased as the Pitt Government had successfully quashed the reform movement in Britain whilst he was in exile. Thomas Muir was the first political martyr to be arrested and brought to trial at the High Court of Justiciary in Edinburgh on the thirtieth of August 1793, charged with promoting and distributing seditious, inflammatory writing 'tending to produce in the minds of the people a spirit of insurrection and of opposition to the established government.' The trial lasted only two days. An accomplished Advocate, Muir conducted his own defence but to no avail. The jurors had been handpicked by the presiding Judge Lord Braxfield and the witnesses for the Crown included Government spies. On pronouncing his guilty sentence, the Lord Justice Clerk (Lord Braxfield) told the court he found Thomas Muir's actions 'heinous ...for it was creating in the lower classes of people, disloyalty and dissatisfaction to government, and this amounting to the highest sort of sedition, is bordering on treason.'

Muir responded to his guilty sentence: 'I have only a few words to say …were I to be led this moment from the bar to scaffold, I should feel the same calmness and serenity which I now do. My mind tells me, that I have acted agreeable to my conscience, and that I have engaged in a good, a just, and a glorious cause – a cause which sooner or later must, and will prevail, and, by a timely reform save this country from destruction." Transported like a felon, he was banished to Botany Bay for fourteen years.

Next came Thomas Fische Palmer, an English Unitarian pastor in Dundee, who was found guilty of sedition by the Circuit Court of Justiciary in Perth on the thirteenth of September, 1793 and sentenced to seven years transportation. Others followed suit. Maurice Margarot and Joseph Gerrald, members of the radical London Corresponding Society were arrested on the second of December 1793 in Edinburgh, charged with sedition by being present at meetings held in Edinburgh late October to discuss political reform. The Instigator of those meetings was William Skirving who was arrested at the same time.

At the conclusion of his two day trial at the High Court of Justiciary in Edinburgh on the sixth and seventh of January 1794 William Skirving, on hearing his guilty sentence for sedition, told the court: "Conscious of innocence, my lords, and that I am not guilty of the crimes laid to my charge, this sentence can only affect me as the sentence of man… I know that what has been done these two days will be rejudged. That is my comfort, and all my hope." All three were sentenced to be transported to Botany Bay for fourteen years.

The Pitt Government persisted in eradicating any discussion on political reform and in 1795 introduced 'gagging' acts – the 'Seditious Meetings Act' and the 'Treason Act.' These acts made speaking or writing about reform a treasonable offence.

Forty years after the date of this novel, Charles Grey, as Prime Minister, was privileged to sit in Parliament to witness the passing of the 1832 Reform Act, a stepping stone in the lengthy pursuit of universal suffrage.

In 1844 a monument to commemorate the five Political Martyrs was erected in the Old Calton Burial Ground in Edinburgh. A tall obelisk, it can be viewed from afar and bears the inscription "…these two days will be rejudged." And they were.

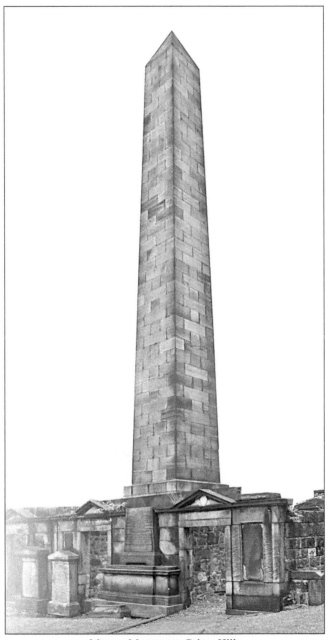

Martyrs Monument, Calton Hill
CC BY-SA 3.0

245